# TAUNTON'S HOME WORKSPACE
# IDEA BOOK

## NEAL ZIMMERMAN

P9-APQ-047

The Taunton Press

EUCLID PUBLIC LIBRARY
631 EAST 222ND STREET
EUCLID, OH 44123
(216) 261-5300

For Smokey, and the big chimney in the sky

Text © 2002 by Neal Zimmerman
Illustrations © 2002 by The Taunton Press, Inc.

All rights reserved.

**The Taunton Press**
Inspiration for hands-on living™

The Taunton Press, Inc., 63 South Main Street, PO Box 5506, Newtown, CT 06470-5506
e-mail: tp@taunton.com

Distributed by Publishers Group West

*Taunton's Home Workspace Idea Book* was originally published in hardcover
as *At Work At Home* in 2001 by The Taunton Press, Inc.


DESIGN: Carol Singer

LAYOUT: Cathy Cassidy

ILLUSTRATOR: Christine Erikson


LIBRARY OF CONGRESS CATALOGING-IN PUBLICATION DATA:
Zimmerman, Neal.
  Taunton's home workspace idea book/ Neal Zimmerman
     p. cm.
  ISBN 1-56158-379-0 hardcover
  ISBN 1-56158-626-9 paperback
   1. Home offices--United States--Design and construction. 2. Office decoration--United
States. I. Title.
  NK2195.O4 Z558 2001
  747.7'3--dc21                                         2001027429

Printed in Singapore
10 9 8 7 6 5 4 3 2 1

# Acknowledgments

First off, kudos to Peter Chapman, senior editor at The Taunton Press, for his superb editorial stewardship of this book throughout the project. Also, thanks to acquisitions editor Steve Culpepper for being the reasonable guy that he is.

AT WORK AT HOME, well over three years in the making, could not have been accomplished without the help of many architects, interior designers, builders, photographers, and home-workplace owners—more than 200 people in all. Although too numerous to mention individually, they deserve credit for contributing their time, talent, great photos, drawings, and fascinating stories about life and work at home.

I especially thank Ed Lang for helping me hold my course through some rough going. And last, I'd like to thank my wife, Leann Sherman, for her good advice and suggestions.

# Contents

# Introduction

▲ This uncluttered work area with a wall of file storage in a converted San Francisco loft is the epitome of a well-organized home workplace.

**W**hen I first started working from home in 1994, I began in what I now call a "first-step home workplace." A lingering recession forced me to consider a less expensive alternative to renting office space, at least for the time being. So I commandeered what was a den on the first floor of our house and moved in office furniture and computer equipment I already owned, shuffling them around to achieve the best fit given the existing conditions of the room. I considered this to be a temporary move. At the time, working out of the house was still regarded by many (including me) as something less than serious.

But a strange thing happened when I got home—I discovered that I was netting more income in less time with less aggravation. This caught my attention. Not surprisingly, literally millions of other people were on the road to a similar discovery.

Although sources vary, it's safe to say that well over 50 million people are now working at home, either full or part time. Tiresome and expensive commutes from home to work,

environmental concerns, and new-age electronic tools have prodded and encouraged many of us to reinvent how, as well as where we work. Research has shown that people can blend work life with home life, while still yielding high levels of productivity, whether for themselves or for their employers. Now, a significant number of corporate employees—so-called telecommuters—also work at home under flexible arrangements. The number of telecommuters totals more than six million. In the very near future, that number is expected to double.

The majority of these people are finding home workplaces to be financially and spiritually successful ventures, leading them to a different and better personal lifestyle. They love working at home, because in addition to saving time and money, they get a huge bonus of personal freedom, which can be invested in relaxation or the achievement of personal goals. They can also spend more time with their children and spouses or provide care for elderly parents. Whereas working at home used to be considered something on the fringe, it has now become desirable, even fashionable. As traditional places of business become more mechanical, metallic, and in some cases almost prison-like, people who work at home are able to generate environments that are softer, mellower, and highly personalized.

Although virtually every home workplace uses one or more personal computers, the home workplace is no longer simply a location for remote keyboard pounding. About a decade into the process, we're seeing a great variety of home-based businesses blooming. Extending far beyond traditional professional service businesses, some home workers have either renovated or built new, small buildings on their home premises to serve the public, operating establishments that run the gamut from retail outlets and miniature fabricating shops to grand-scale aerobics gymnasia.

People often begin working at home on a temporary or trial basis, sometimes because of a personal or financial need. At first, the decor may be modest—a card table, a folding chair, or a desk found in the attic shoehorned into the corner of a bedroom. But for the long term, first-step home workplaces are often unpleasant, poorly functional, and unhealthful. That's because many of the estimated 50 million home workers—who wouldn't think of planning a kitchen without an experienced kitchen designer—cobble together home workplaces without any professional help, relying solely on their intuition and leftover furnishings. But as more of us

▲ **Working at home is not a new idea. This restored farm manager's home office, which dates from the late 19th century, was where the owner caught up on office work at night. Sound familiar?**

◀Working at home gives you the opportunity to personalize your workplace with objects that have interest and meaning for you.

begin working at home, we are now recognizing the need for good home workplace design.

## ABOUT THIS BOOK

In the process of converting the family den to my first home workplace in 1994, I was able to borrow on 25 years of experience as a corporate workplace designer and architect. I hope to lend you some of this experience as well. I'll begin by outlining basic workplace planning principles. I'll show you how to take stock of your needs, how to evaluate and choose a location, and how to develop a home workplace that helps you balance your work style and home life.

After reviewing basic concepts, I'll examine a variety of home workplaces of myriad sizes and styles, focusing on the planning and thinking that went into the design. I'll start with what I call shared spaces, for those who have only limited space available. Because shared spaces offer little or no separation

from the overall living space, I'll show you how some people turned an alcove or a even a closet into a slightly more privatized home workplace, or niche.

If you have a room somewhere that you're able to call your own, whether it be a basement space, garage, bedroom, den, or attic, I'll show you many fine examples of how to convert and dedicate that space for home-workplace use. If you've got an itch to build

▲A sunny parlor in a remodeled Victorian townhouse becomes an artistic and playful workspace for an interior designer.

out, I'll walk you through several additions, renovated outbuildings, and new workplaces that were designed from the ground up. And if you expect business activities to include regular visitors, such as clients, students, or customers, I'll show you workplaces that were successfully developed for going public.

Whereas five years ago excellent examples were hard to come by, we're finally seeing a host of marvelous home/work environments—of all shapes, sizes, styles, and persuasions. I've chosen to show examples that are organized sensibly, that have a design spirit about them, and that work efficiently for the functions intended. I've also tried to choose examples whose designs should wear well over time, regardless of changes in computers and other high-tech gadgets that find their way into the home workplace. In our travels, we'll wander through well over 200 home workplaces—from minuscule and modest to spacious and majestic—stretching from the windswept dunes of Cape Cod through the expanse of the Midwest to the sunny beaches of Malibu. Along the way, we'll even stop by my own second-generation home workplace for a short visit.

The varied photo examples I've assembled for this book have one thing in common—they represent more for their inhabitants than merely a place to suffer work. There's a personality about them: to paraphrase Gertrude Stein, "There's a *there* there." As we move from

▲ The availability of affordable computers and communications equipment is one of the driving forces behind the work-at-home phenomenon.

one example to the next, I'll focus on specific design details that make each space work, helping you to visualize and perhaps materialize aspects for your own home workplace.

Experience changes perception. Working at home has proven to be more than a fad, and there's an emerging awareness that the quality of the home workplace counts—not only for efficiency, comfort, and safety, but for the sheer pleasure of being there. Home workplaces are beginning to enjoy the respect afforded other key spaces in the home—so that in addition to getting work done productively, we can also spend our time there peacefully and joyously. Let's now see how the dream can become reality.

# First Steps

Nowadays, it seems as though everyone's getting into the work-at-home habit. Whether it's bringing work home to keep up with a heavy office load, telecommuting to corporate HQ a couple of days a week, or running a home-based business, working at home is here to stay.

It's one thing to make the decision to work at home, but quite another to create a home workplace that's just right for you. Not so many years ago, a home work space meant little more than a couch in the living room or a card table or hand-me-down desk tucked in the corner of the bedroom. Not anymore. Makeshift workstations are giving way to a variety of well-equipped spaces that are specifically designed for their occupants' work requirements and neatly woven into the fabric of their homes.

Why do some of these spaces work and others fall short? I've reviewed hundreds of home workplaces, and I've concluded that those that are the most successful have three basic features in common. First, they help their occupants *balance the two sides of their lives*—work life and home life—in a way that is harmonious not just for them, but also for the people with whom they share their living and working space. Second, the workplace is *well planned and well organized;* it allows the user to work in a "CEO" environment—that is, with Comfort, Efficiency, and Organization. Third, a successful home workplace has a *personal spirit about it*, which is a reflection of its occupant. It's this personal spirit that stimulates home workers to do their best work.

◄One of the main benefits of working at home is that you can create an environment that's conducive to productivity. A great view doesn't hurt, either. This well-organized, second-floor architect's studio for two looks out over the Atlantic Ocean.

◄A successful home workplace helps its user harmoniously balance work life and home life. This second-floor workplace looks out onto the living room below, providing a strong sense of connection with the rest of the house. At the same time, the solid half-wall screens the workstation from below, thereby visually privatizing the work area.

▼More than just a place to work at home, this boldly colored sunroom alcove is an expression of the personality of the owner.

These three basic features are more easily rattled off than they are accomplished. Creating a successful home workplace is an involved process that requires good design intelligently integrated with fundamental workplace planning principles. It's the successful marriage of space and function, with a carefully developed plan for getting it all done, that makes the difference between a wonderful place to work and a disorganized, half-baked setup.

So, how do you get there and where do you start? As you plan your own home workplace and sort through the myriad ideas and examples put forth in this and

▲Well-planned drawers, storage cubbies, and bookshelves are synonymous with organization and efficiency, hallmarks of a successful home workplace. In this shared space, the execution of the design is simple and the result elegant.

later chapters, the process can get confusing. Furthermore, I know you're very busy working to pay for, among other things, this new home workplace. So I'm going to keep it as simple as I can. I've come up with five basic steps for successful home workplace planning. As you contemplate your own workplace and begin to make decisions about what you like and what might work for you, bear these steps in mind:

1. Know your needs.
2. Choose your location carefully.
3. Develop a floor plan that meets your needs in your chosen location.
4. Create a comfortable and healthy environment.
5. Design a place that feels just right for you, a place for who you are.

## 10 Questions to Ask Yourself Before Setting Up a Home Workplace

1. What do I produce, and how much space will I need to do it?
2. Will I need any help in the form of employees?
3. Do I expect to have visitors, and, if so, where will I meet them?
4. How will the work I do, and the place where I choose to do it, affect the other members of my household?
5. Will I be able to successfully privatize my workplace to accommodate my business needs and also avoid disruptions?
6. Will there be enough space for storage and conferencing?
7. Will there be adequate utilities—enough power, lighting, and heating/cooling—to satisfy my personal and equipment needs? If not, can they be made available?
8. Do I have a clear idea of how much it will cost, in time and money, to get my home work place prepared as required?
9. Do I need approvals from local authorities to use or modify my workplace as intended?
10. Where do I turn for professional help if I need it?

If you follow these steps, you'll develop a workplace that really works. Let's look at these steps in a little more detail.

## Know Your Needs

Before you begin to even think of choosing a location for your home workplace, it's critical to have a clear idea of your requirements of operation. To guide you in this preliminary process, I've drawn up a list of 10 questions that you should ask yourself before setting up a home workplace (see the sidebar at left).

### The Three Elements of Control

One of the key words to remember when you start planning your home workplace is control. When you work at home, it's imperative that you exercise three elements of control over your work environment. You'll need *privacy*, or the ability to work without interruption; you'll need to provide *protection* for your workplace and all of its paraphernalia from marauding family members (and pets); and if you expect to have visitors or staff, you'll somehow need to develop *separation* between business traffic and family living space. For example, a spare bedroom may offer privacy and protection, but it won't necessarily give you the separation you need if you plan to have clients or staff.

If all homes could accommodate it, every home workplace would have its own entry

▲ If you anticipate that visitors or clients will come to your home workplace, you'll need a room or a separate space where you can meet them. In this California home office, conference space is separated from the main production area on a mezzanine accessed by an elegant stairway.

and the work space would be dedicated just for work. If you can swing it, this is clearly the way to go. But for many people, especially those who are just starting out on the work-at-home adventure, it will be a while before they can or wish to consider allocating or creating dedicated space. At least for the present, space will have to be shared with home life in some fashion—in a bedroom or family room, a converted closet, or perhaps even a wide hallway.

**Creating privacy and protection** No matter what the configuration or size of your home, you are going to need privacy and protection to work effectively. Fortunately,

▲ If space is tight and you don't expect visitors, a workstation in a hallway may be all you need. This desk alcove in a hallway between the kitchen and guest bedroom suite offers a modicum of separation from the main living areas of the house.

this can be achieved in varying degrees, without complete physical separation of the work space from the rest of the home.

Depending upon your particular home layout and family situation, the ability to create privacy will vary from easy to unmanageable. If you live alone, privacy may simply mean that you shut off the television and get to work. In a family situation where you are sharing space in a bedroom or den, privacy becomes something that needs to be

negotiated, scheduled, or worked out by whatever it takes to achieve a mutually acceptable solution, when walls and doors aren't available to do the job.

To protect your workplace in a shared situation, you'll have to establish your own territory. The best protection is to be able to close it off from the rest of the shared space. That's one reason why closet conversions are popular. If you can't close off your work area, you still need to establish your own

◄In a shared space, setting up a folding screen between the workplace and the living area provides visual privacy for the user.

territory, even if it's just a small corner of the shared room that is dedicated to you and your work. If you can manage to visually separate your work area by repositioning a bookcase or even setting up a folding screen, it will provide some visual privacy and more clearly establish territory. It also helps to have everything in your area of command well organized and stowed, which prevents spillover into neighboring territory and vice versa.

In most cases, children will present the greatest challenge to sharing work space within living space. In some instances, there's no practical way to satisfy both needs, but each situation is unique, and ultimately you'll have to be the judge. No matter what your living circumstances, privacy and protection issues will have to be resolved for you to work successfully.

**Creating a sense of separation** A home workplace that welcomes clients or staff requires more clearly defined elements of

▲The best protection for your work space in a shared situation is being able to close it off from the rest of the room. When work is done for the day in this New York apartment, the keyboard tray rolls into the narrow, converted closet and the door slides across to conceal the workstation. When the closet is closed, all that's left is an office chair that can be rolled under the window work surface to the left. In shutdown mode, the room serves double duty as a guest bedroom.

separation. Business visitors expect and deserve to have their business relationship with you kept distinct from your personal and family life. For example, you may have plenty of extra space within your bedroom to set up a work area with a little conference table, but a bedroom isn't an appropri-

# Swing Spaces, Meeting Places

Not all workplaces are large enough or appropriate for client meetings. If you've chosen to do your work in a shared bedroom or in a dedicated space within your bedroom quarters, or if workplace access is through personal living space, you should consider alternative locations for meetings.

The two most common alternatives are "swing spaces" and remote locations. Swing space is space that is ordinarily used for other home functions, such as a dining room, a family study, or a room located near an entry. If the room is neat, well organized, and "interruption-proof," it's perfectly appropriate to conduct small meetings of short duration there.

For longer or larger meetings, it's better to schedule them at a remote location. In the case of formal meetings with several clients, it's a good idea to investigate renting space on

▲ A small dining area off the kitchen serves as "swing space" for occasional meetings. This well-lit space has the added advantage of direct entry from outside, which means that visitors don't have to pass through personal living areas of the house.

an hourly basis. Some office-rental companies can offer fully equipped conference rooms by the hour or half-day. For less formal meetings, a coffeehouse or bookstore cafe should work just fine.

ate place to host a client or accommodate staff, no matter how large it is or how nicely it is designed and maintained.

Beyond the taboos, your image is also important. Although it's accepted that the home workplace is, in general, a more relaxed atmosphere, a lack of separation between family members, personal spaces,

and business visitors puts your seriousness and professionalism into question.

That said, a space embedded within the fabric of the family homestead can still work for you if you don't have staff, and if you can confer with an occasional visitor in a "swing space" location near the entry, perhaps in a den or dining room.

◀An L-shaped workstation arrangement provides for two distinct work areas—computer and administrative. The administrative desk surface, unobstructed by equipment, is placed at the view.

## How Much Space Do You Need?

Perhaps the most difficult need to assess is the amount of space you'll require, which can vary dramatically from one type of home business to the next. As a starting point for assessing space needs, I've developed an acronym that many people have found helpful. I call it "CAMP."

"C" is for Computer stations, one or more of which will be found in virtually every home workplace today, no matter what type of work you do. "A" stands for the Administrative station—the place where you open your mail, pay bills, prepare packages for mailing, and perhaps take telephone calls. "M" is the Meeting station, which may vary from none at all

▲Project and administrative stations sit side-by-side in this architect's second-floor home workplace. The administrative station commands the view outside, while the project station overlooks the first-floor living areas through a wide, screenable opening. A movable tool storage caddy is accessible when needed and rolled under when not in use.

► Workstations don't have to be in a contiguous space. This project station for a home florist is in a converted two-car garage. Administrative work is done at a small work space within the house.

▲ In this freestanding studio workplace on Nantucket Island, computer, administrative, and project stations occupy the second floor, while the meeting station and reception area are downstairs, close to the entry. The storefront glass at the conference area can be protected by wide storm doors.

to a significant-size conference table. And "P" stands for Project station, which is the most variable type in size, equipment, and number. Clearly, a floral arranger will need a different project station than a woodworker, a fine artist, or a computer-software designer will require.

Not everyone will need all four station types. In some cases, two or even three of these functions can overlap at a single station—again, depending upon your specific needs. Plus the stations don't all have to be in one contiguous space; an example of this would be a spare bedroom workplace where you would conduct remote conferencing.

# It's Not Just an Office Anymore

Think "home workplace" and most people picture an office setup of some kind. But as the work-at-home movement gathers pace, we're seeing all types of businesses operated from home. Some receive a significant number of visitors daily (such as the aerobics instructor and decoy maker featured in "Going Public" on p. 220). Other home-business operators require specialized spaces for their particular equipment (such as cabinetmakers and sculptors, weavers, and quilters).

Needless to say, the workplace requirements of these specialized home businesses are very specific to individual circumstances. Your business, your land and home, your financial situation, and local ordinances will all have to be examined carefully in order to create a successful work environment. Before you start shelling out money or breaking ground for a new building, it's important to seek preliminary opinions and guidance from everybody who'll lend you an ear—including your lawyer, accountant, banker, building department, and an architect.

▲ Not everyone who works at home sits at a desk all day, but issues of privacy, protection, and separation are still important. Here, a weaver has set up shop in a lower-level room four steps down from the main level and separated from the living area by a half-wall.

## Assessing Your Storage Needs

Your storage needs will vary depending upon the kind of work you do. Take an inventory of all records, supplies, perhaps even products, and determine a rough calculation of how much storage space you need. Bear in mind that not everything has to be stored in one place.

# Storage: Active, Inactive, or Dead?

There are three types of storage. The first is *active storage*—materials you need access to on a regular basis, such as documents, files, and supplies. The second is *inactive storage*—stuff you'll occasionally need to access, like bulk supplies, completed client records, or reference books. The third is *dead storage*—that's the stuff you need to bury, once and for all. Either find an out-of-the-way place to keep the files or throw them out.

Because storage space is usually at a premium in a home workplace, you can't afford to have inactive storage taking up valuable real estate there. Look for dry, accessible space elsewhere in the home, such as in an attic

▲Shelves and cabinets on the three sides of this U-shaped workstation provide active and accessible storage for the many books this writer requires. The credenza behind offers additional storage just a short chair roll away.

or basement. A word of caution: Certain kinds of records and many kinds of supplies do not store well in hot or moist locations. Be sure to consider this before placing sensitive items in peril.

Over time, inactive storage expands, and you'll need to sort through it periodically to see what can be moved to the dead storage category. It's a good idea to catalog your inactive storage items on a computer file to prevent wasted trips and frustrating searches in the storage area. File boxes should be identified and put on shelves, to avoid having to shuffle heavy boxes in cramped or uncomfortable locations.

▲Active storage should be readily accessible to the workstation. Here, a lateral file drawer stores documents below the computer station work surface. The porpoise hardware adds a playful touch.

▲Inactive storage was moved to an unused extra bathroom that was modified to store reference books and old plans.

▲A rest room close to your workplace is a welcome convenience. If you have clients or a staff, a separate rest room is a virtual necessity, preferably close to an entrance, as shown here.

## Do You Need to Add a Rest Room?

If you work alone or with a family member, you can simply use the rest room facilities in your living quarters. However, if you expect to receive visitors or clients or if you have employees, you'll need to add at least one accessible rest room to avoid potential cross-traffic problems. It's not appropriate for visitors or staff to regularly march through your living quarters. Check regulations for barrier-free design requirements.

You'll have to provide room for things you use regularly, within or very near your workplace (active storage). Excess supplies and older records and papers (inactive storage) can be stored elsewhere, even at a remote storage location. And remember, in an efficient and productive home workplace, there's one place that's off limits for storage. You guessed it: the floor.

## Assessing Your Energy Needs

Your new home workplace will require power for equipment and machinery, adequate lighting, and low-voltage communications links for your telephone and perhaps for your computer or television. All this stuff creates heat, which will have an impact on ventilation and cooling, yet another energy requirement. When everything is tallied, you may find that you need to expand your heating and/or cooling system, or perhaps get a standalone system for your chosen workplace.

Although more low-voltage wiring (for networks, cable, etc.) is slithering itself into the walls of our homes, desktop equipment is becoming smaller, multifunctional, and simplified, requiring less space, power, and

# Permission to Work at Home

Before you make a commitment to working at home, find out whether you can operate legally in your specific location. These days, many local jurisdictions and community associations require you to apply for a permit if you plan to work at home. If you'll be working solo and you don't create any noise or waste, you'll most likely be granted permission.

If you intend to have employees or to host visitors, getting permission may be more involved. For one thing, certain cities and towns simply prohibit business operations at home. And even if home businesses are permitted as-of-right, parking and building-safety issues may come into play. Local officials want to be sure that you don't create a nuisance for the community at large or endanger other people. They may also be empowered to have a say about whether or where you display a business sign.

Town ordinances are quite explicit about where and in what kind of buildings certain types of business will be permitted, especially those that operate machinery, deal with volatile sub-stances, or create significant or hazardous waste. When hazardous waste is mentioned, most of us think of dangerous chemicals, but even sawdust or paint can be an environmental or personal health concern.

The penalty for ignoring local ordinances and requirements can be severe. There's no sense spending time and money to get started, only to be ordered to shut down later. Therefore, it's imperative that you check with local governing bodies to be sure you can set up a home workplace.

▲ If you operate a home-based business and you receive visitors, the local authorities may require you to add parking spaces to satisfy customer needs. They may also regulate the type and size of sign you may use.

protection than equipment of the very recent past. Although obviously important, machinery continues to become less imposing, and as a result, we can turn our attention more freely to the way in which our home workplace is designed—for our benefit, rather than simply for the benefit of the machines.

Nevertheless, it's all got to be considered beforehand and provided for in your new workplace, with associated costs. It may also take some time and construction in order to get these support elements in place.

It's a good idea to take an inventory of energy needs by creating a list of all the equipment you expect to use, as well as the power requirements for each. When you get to choosing a location, and if your requirements are significant, you may want to review your list with an architect or engineer, who can help you determine what's feasible and help you estimate costs for additional power or systems.

## Choose Your Location

Once you have a clear idea of your workplace needs, the next step is to determine where in your house to set up shop. Choosing a location for a home workplace is a matter of accommodating your work needs and your control requirements with the available space.

If you're lucky, you have a spare bedroom, an existing study, or a convenient hideaway that can be converted quickly and painlessly. Failing that, maybe there's a suit-

▲ Built in the style of the original owner's favorite French château, this ribbed-arch second-floor space started out as a billiard room and later saw service as a children's theater, complete with elevated stage. Now it's reborn as the perfect setting for a dedicated home workplace.

◄The view and access to the exterior and the soaring clerestory space make this room hard to pass up for use as either a bedroom or a workplace. In this case, it's used as both. The matching wood trim and workstation materials help make the workplace appear to be more than a thrown-in afterthought.

location can be so uncomfortable or unworkable as to cause the entire effort to fail.

In this section, we'll look briefly at the various locations that might be considered as potential workplaces and consider the benefits and detriments of each. In subsequent chapters, we'll examine the location options in greater depth.

## Shared Spaces

Shared spaces are workplace locations in rooms or other open spaces that serve double duty—sometimes as a workplace and at other times as a living space for you or your family.

**Workplace/Bedroom combo** A tempting location for setting up a home workplace is in a master bedroom. It is typically one of the larger rooms in the house and is relatively isolated from the public living space. The room is finished, usually has natural

able location that hadn't previously crossed your mind, such as an attic, basement, garage, or outbuilding. Perhaps you'll have to consider the pros and cons of sharing space in a room that has to accommodate other household functions. Maybe you're thinking about an addition.

The arrangement that's best for you will depend upon the kind of work you do, the characteristics of your home, your family arrangement, and your budget. Your choice will be the single most important decision you'll make about your home workplace. Whether you are telecommuting or operating a home-based business, a poorly chosen light and good ventilation, and may have a good view. What's more, the bedroom is often unused during the day.

The problem with setting up your workplace in a bedroom is that there are too many potential distractions. Even if you live alone, working where you sleep requires strong personal discipline. It's too tempting to leave the television on or the bed unmade. If someone else sleeps there with you, working in the bedroom may stretch the sharing concept beyond the breaking point.

If the master bedroom isn't an option as a shared workplace, consider using a spare/guest bedroom (if you're fortunate enough to have one). Setting up a workplace in a spare bedroom has all the advan-

tages of the master bedroom option, but it's a lot less disruptive of home life. After all, this is probably a room that's used only a few nights a year.

**Gathering rooms** Otherwise known as living rooms, family rooms, or dens, these spaces are worth considering for use as a shared workplace. Gathering rooms are usually large and near an entry, so you might be able to cordon off a section, screen it, and have a semi-private workplace from which you can greet occasional visitors.

▲ One approach to blending work life with home life in a shared space is to surround modern electronic gear with well-chosen antique furniture.

◀ In a shared space, a flair for organization helps to prevent spillover into neighboring territory. This custom-made modular workstation tucked into a living room features twin storage towers with large numbers for handles. More than just a design statement, the numbered handles are also the key to a filing system.

◀This simple period kitchen workstation is an ideal spot for making quick notes and grocery lists. Workplaces that receive anything more than light-duty use for short duration will need more space and better separation from the heart of a kitchen.

One of the main problems with gathering space is just that—families tend to want to gather there, which could invite interruptions and distractions. These rooms are commonly (but not always) near central paths of circulation in the home, which can cause privacy and separation problems, especially if there are young children in the house.

Family rooms are often open to spaces such as stairways or kitchens, which tend to receive a lot of family traffic and generate a lot of noise. It may be possible to arrange the family room to serve double duty by screening off an area for workplace use or by constructing a divider that can serve as workplace on one side, entertainment center on the other.

**Kitchen** The kitchen table has been the birthplace of many home-based businesses, but it's not a location I recommend for anything other than a temporary workplace. Although a kitchen is a tempting location to begin working at home as a "freebie," because there's a table and telephone already in place, the demands on a kitchen don't mix well with workplace use.

I've seen some very attractive little spaces designed inside kitchens, but unless they support a kitchen-related business, they don't stand up comfortably to shared use. Aside from the typical distractions, you'll probably have to put a lot of materials, equipment, and functions somewhere else, which reduces efficiency beyond the level of practicality.

## Niche Spaces

Niche spaces are a step up from shared spaces in that they offer a little more protection and sometimes a little more privacy. Spaces that fall into this category include nooks and alcoves off a larger room, closets, stairwells and hallways, and lofts. These spaces can work well for people with modest space requirements.

Niche spaces that can be closed off (such as an alcove separated from a larger room with pocket doors) are particularly effective

◄This workplace in an alcove off the main living area can be privatized by closing the pocket doors. In a work space without a wall window, the central skylight brings in natural light and also makes the space seem larger.

## Screening Your Workplace

If you live in a loft space or in a home with a large family room or bedroom, you might be able to screen off a portion of the space for your workplace. Curtains, blinds, or a strategically placed privacy screen can clearly, but simply, enclose a space. Alternatively, an arrangement of furniture or storage units might do the trick. For a more permanent solution, a half-height wall can achieve similar results (see the top photo and floor plan on p. 51).

Any of these arrangements will give you visual privacy and some additional territorial control. An advantage of this setup compared to an open shared space is that you don't have to put everything away each time you stop work to make the rest of the room more habitable as living space.

because the doors afford you visual privacy and a fair measure of sound control. Closets are popular locations for compact home workplaces because they offer protection and can be closed off when not in use. The most common conversion is of a shallow, but wide closet with bifold doors. If you're fortunate to have a walk-in closet that you can spare, it could also be converted to a suitable small workplace with some minor modifications (see chapter 3 for more details). In most cases, a closet will have to be wired for electricity and communications.

► Dead space under a stair can be used as a small workstation or, as here, for storage. In this loft in a converted San Francisco brewery, the custom-built stepped *tansu* chest mimics the stainless-steel staircase above and provides storage for standard-size files, office equipment, and a fax machine.

▲ A landing at the top of the stairs is just wide enough to accommodate a built-in desk and allow passage to second-floor bedrooms. The narrow end wall to the left and the sloped back wall, which is the underside of a ship's ladder to the attic above, provide a sense of enclosure.

Spaces under a stair, which may be underutilized or not even used at all, can be reclaimed for a small utility work space or for storage (see the drawing on p. 85). Although there may be limited angular space above the work counter, a clever arrangement can pack in a lot of stuff in a small space. You might also consider setting up a small workstation on a wide stair landing.

The advantage of using a hallway for a workplace niche is that you don't have to share the space as you would in a bedroom or family room. But it isn't completely private, because family members will have to pass through the workplace area. This is a privacy issue you'll have to handle with diplomacy rather than drywall. Protection may also be an issue, depending upon your family; this can be addressed with drawers and cabinets.

▲ Careful selection of furnishings and artwork in this redefined space helps eliminate the bedroom-like feel that can remain in many a converted spare bedroom.

## Redefined Spaces

If you feel that a shared space or a niche space won't give you adequate privacy (or enough room) for a home workplace, the next step is to assess whether there are any locations in your home that are going unused. Potential spots include spare bedrooms, dining rooms, and dens, as well as spaces outside the main living areas of the house—attics, basements, sunrooms, and garages. Depending on the location you choose, these spaces will require different levels of preparation for use—anything from minor alterations to major overhauls.

**Bedroom conversion** A spare or guest bedroom is an excellent place to set up a home

workplace for privacy and protection, though not necessarily for separation. Smaller bedrooms are suitable for one-person offices; larger bedrooms can be configured for two people. Bedrooms (and dining rooms and dens) are already largely prepared to function as a workplace: They're most likely insulated and have power, lighting, as well as a window or two. Bedroom closets can be converted for storage.

If the spare bedroom is isolated from other bedrooms and can be accessed easily from the entry, it might even afford you the separation you need to have visitors or an assistant. On the other hand, if the bedroom is contiguous with other family bedrooms, it

◀This basement workplace is well integrated with the rest of the lower level. In a wall workstation arrangement, the upper wall can be pressed into service for storage.

▼Here's an antidote for the cold, damp basement space: a highly personalized half-basement workplace, with large windows, mirrored surfaces, carpeting, and a playful color scheme. The designer has come up with a creative solution for concealing the electrical pipe that runs around the room—turning it into a chair rail that divides the white and pink sections of the wall.

will present the same separation problems as mentioned previously.

**Basement conversion** Unfinished basements are typically large, open spaces that are often underutilized, which makes them attractive candidates for home workplaces. Electrical panels and heating systems are commonly located in basements, so the cost of distributing power and heat is minimized. Walk-out basements offer the additional advantage of a connection with the outdoors along with some natural light. In some cases, the doorway may also be used as a dedicated entry to the home workplace, which offers separation from the living quarters above.

That's the good news. But there are a lot of other things to consider before you turn your basement into your workplace. Full basements that receive little or no daylight are not the best places to be working eight hours a day. Most of these have tiny windows that don't let in much natural light,

▲Attics don't have to be dark and dingy workplaces. With a vaulted ceiling, large windows, and added skylight, this attic studio above a garage is transformed into an open and airy workplace. The operable skylight helps reduce heat buildup.

are too high to provide a view, and may be too small for safe egress in case of an emergency—something that your local building department might also be concerned about. Headroom in basements may be a problem, as may dampness and water penetration. You may also have to finish your basement, which could mean constructing partitions, adding doors, installing flooring, and introducing lighting.

**Attic conversion** Like basements, attics are often underused extra space. Their remote location ensures privacy and protection for

your workplace but may present an access problem for visitors and staff. Attics tend to stay dry (although heat buildup can be a problem); they often have interesting pitched ceilings, which can be enhanced with skylights; and a well-placed window might give you a commanding bird's-eye view. Not coincidentally, this is the place where I chose to locate my own home workplace (see p. 112).

Attic spaces often require a full construction program in order to make them habitable. For example, some attics don't have enough height between floor and roof to

## Adding an Attic Dormer

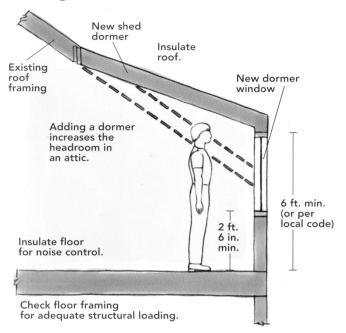

New shed dormer

Insulate roof.

Existing roof framing

New dormer window

Adding a dormer increases the headroom in an attic.

Insulate floor for noise control.

Check floor framing for adequate structural loading.

2 ft. 6 in. min.

6 ft. min. (or per local code)

provide adequate clearance. This can be remedied in a number of ways, the most common of which is to add a dormer (see the drawing at left). In other attics, the existing floor may not be strong enough to handle the additional live loads imposed by the new use, in which case you'll need to beef up the floor framing. You'll also need to make sure there's a window opening large enough (by code) from which to escape in case of fire. If you have any doubt about these conditions, make sure you seek professional advice from an architect or engineer before laying claim to the attic as your new workplace home.

### Sunroom conversion

Sunrooms (and porches) can make excellent home offices, not least because they're connected to the outdoors on two or three sides. They're usually just

◄With views on two or three sides, sunrooms are excellent candidates for conversion to workplaces. But direct sunlight and high-summer heat can be too much of a good thing, so it's important to install shades that can be dropped as required.

about the right size for a one-person workplace, and because of their location it's often possible to give them a separate entry. Sunrooms and screened porches will have to be insulated, enclosed, and supplied with power and temperature conditioning.

Sunrooms are designed to maximize sunlight. Natural light is a good thing, but too much of it creates glare and heat buildup. Be sure that you consider this issue carefully before converting a sunroom into a home workplace. (For more on sunroom conversions, see p. 120.)

**Garage conversion** Garage conversions offer great potential, because they can provide a separate exterior entrance to the new home workplace. There are a number of other positives to using a garage, which include the possibility of adding skylights, opening up the ceiling to create a vaulted space, and providing views to the yard through newly introduced windows. If you decide to use your garage, you'll lose covered and protected parking. The question then becomes what to do with the car, the lawn mower, and so forth. Before you get too serious about this option, check with the local authorities to see if they'll allow you to make this conversion.

Not unlike an unfinished basement, a garage will involve a considerable amount of construction to prepare it for workplace

▲ A converted garage provides just enough room for a project area for a quilter's home-based business. The garage door was replaced with a large three-light, insulated window, bringing in lots of natural light and a great view.

activities. You'll also most likely have a concrete slab that slopes slightly toward the overhead door. This should be insulated and leveled (see the drawing on p. 173).

## Renovated Outbuildings

If your search for a suitable location within the home comes up short, perhaps you are lucky enough to have a shed, barn, or other outbuilding on your property that could be converted to a workplace. Bear in mind, however, that renovations and adaptive reuse of older existing structures can be quite complex. They may involve jacking up the building, pouring a new foundation, upgrading the existing structure and roof, sup-

► A three-story library addition includes space for a home workplace on the second floor. The ground level, conveniently accessed from the street, serves as a meeting room and family den.

plying power and utilities from the main building, and perhaps even eliminating hazardous materials, such as asbestos shingles or ground contaminants.

Renovating an outbuilding can be even more complicated than starting from scratch, and many different approvals may be required. This kind of work is the topic of many other books, but the basic planning issues for creating a home workplace within a converted outbuilding remain the same as for any other space.

## Additions and Freestanding Structures

Building an addition or a freestanding structure is an expensive option (and not one that everybody has), but it offers the greatest benefits. First, to state the obvious, this is additional space, as opposed to space borrowed from somewhere else. Second, even though there may be limitations, you have significantly more design latitude when you have control over the building envelope. Last but not least, you'll be able to create a separate entrance, which is always a plus for a home workplace.

◀A 10-ft. by 10-ft. music shed built on a tight urban lot in San Francisco packs in space for recording equipment, a sitting area, and storage for records and a collection of guitars—all against the backdrop of a beautifully landscaped rear yard.

▼A copper-sided art studio on concrete piers seems to float in the woods in this gently sloping rear yard. The entry faces away from the house and into the woods, ensuring privacy and a distinct separation between work and home.

Additions will require two different but related forms of approval. The first is approval to operate your kind of business at home. For example, zoning regulations might prohibit it, or perhaps your particular business will require off-street parking, which may not available. The second is approval to build the addition itself. Setback requirements, maximum building size on a given lot, and utility easements may prohibit you from moving forward with a building addition. It's imperative that you check out these two approval issues with local planning officials before you do anything else. Should you get through the approval stage, you'll next have to get some planning help, and then live through what most people consider to be the worst part of the whole process: construction.

A freestanding structure is the ultimate home workplace—a workplace away from home that's still home. Building a freestanding structure will require adequate land, even more stringent approvals than an addition, detailed design plans, and a significant amount of time and money in order to realize the dream.

# Sketching a Plan

The first step is to create a background drawing. Measure the area or room you've chosen, wall by wall, and then transfer it in scale onto a sheet of graph paper. Draw in the doors, windows, radiators, and any other landmark features or obstructions in the space, including electrical outlets and switches. Designers call this a background plan, because it will serve as the background for your alternate layout sketches.

The second step is to develop a two-dimensional plan. It's a good idea to photocopy the background plan several times. Then you can sketch work surfaces, furniture, and equipment right on a copy, preferably in a different color. An alternative is to sketch on tracing paper over the background. You can also use a simple computer drafting application to do all this work.

Success in developing a floor plan will require a very accurate background plan, as well as a thorough knowledge of your workstation, equipment, and storage needs. You might even generate two or three alternate plans to see which one works the best. After deciding on the preferred layout, you can then think about your power requirements—where you'll need to introduce outlets, phone jacks, and so on.

## Developing the Plan

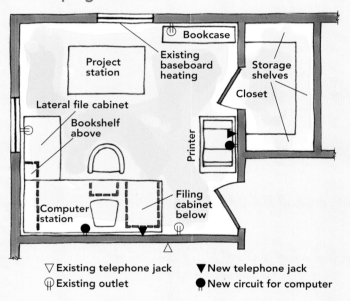

▽ Existing telephone jack  ▼ New telephone jack
⌾ Existing outlet  ● New circuit for computer

Assuming that you've got the land and it's buildable, bear in mind that this is a new building from the ground up—which means excavation, foundations, roofing, framing, utility supply, and all new systems before you even get to the interior of the home workplace. It's quite an undertaking, but the prize is great. Just take a look at some of the finished workplaces at the end of this book. At one time, all they had was a dream like yours.

## Develop a Floor Plan

You've carefully analyzed your needs, and you've selected a location in your home that you believe will meet your requirements.

►When developing a floor plan, experiment with different workstation arrangements to see which fits the space best. A corner layout allows space to either side of a computer workstation and is particularly effective in a small room. Custom cabinets maximize use of the space.

Now it's time to test that location, to see if everything will fit, and to get an idea of what will be involved to make the space work for you. In order to do this with any sense of conviction, at minimum you'll have to develop a two-dimensional floor plan. Some people are capable of making this drawing themselves, and for them I'll provide some general advice (see the sidebar on the facing page). For those of you who are not so inclined, I suggest you enlist the help of a designer or architect, who in most cases can develop a basic floor plan for you at a modest cost.

For many people, developing a floor plan is the most difficult part of the whole process, because it involves not only a skilled inventory of needs but also an ability to think and plan on paper. People who jump in headlong without a plan typically run into problems and get hit with unexpected costs, which sometimes escalate beyond affordability. What's worse, they rarely get where they intended to go because they began their journey without a map or directional compass.

## Before You Build, Get Help

If you're planning an addition or a new building for your home workplace, you should seriously consider hiring an architect to develop drawings and specifications for you. Here are a few reasons why:

- You get the benefit of professional design experience.
- You can discuss details with the architect before construction begins, which is always better than having to make decisions while tradesmen are on the job.
- You have drawings to submit to the building department, which may be a requirement where you live.
- You can expect some standard of expectation, which the contractor will be obliged to meet, during construction.
- You can develop an independent cost estimate, which will serve as a basis of comparison when assessing bids from contractors.

## Sample Workstation Arrangements

**STRAIGHT**

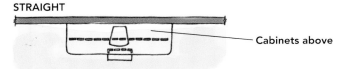

Cabinets above

**CORNER**

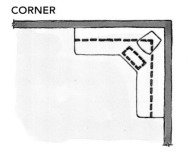

**U-SHAPED**

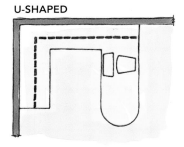

**GALLEY**

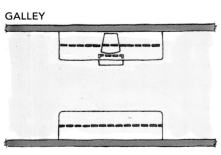

**ALCOVE**

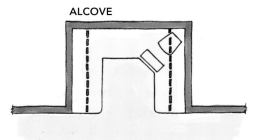

**CLOSET**

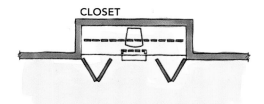

Once you've developed a plan, not only will you have a preview of your workplace but you'll also be able to estimate the cost. Using the plan, get prices from reliable contractors or subcontractors; in order to work out the total budget, don't forget to add in the cost of furniture, built-ins, and any new equipment.

# Create the Right Environment

It's not enough just to pour money into a construction project and create a dramatic space. You need to make it comfortable— and that takes more than studs, drywall, and expensive finishes. It means thinking about lighting, views, and comfortable seating and ergonomic tools.

## Lighting

It's desirable to have natural light in a home workplace, mainly because it provides a view and a connection to outdoors. But even if natural light streams into your workplace, there are a couple of reasons to introduce artificial light. First, light varies depending upon weather, time of day, and time of year. Second, there may be times when you need to shade natural light because of glare or heat gain.

Generally speaking, lighting falls into two categories: ambient or task. If you think of a garden hose, the wide-spray position of

▲Selection and arrangement of lighting requires careful thinking. Inappropriate positioning of equipment or choices of lighting may produce unwanted reflections on monitors, direct eye glare, or inadequate amounts of coverage or brightness on work surfaces. Here, a simple task light illuminates the computer workstation.

▲Built-in fluorescent lighting under the bottom shelves at work-surface level lights the niches that house equipment. Baffled fluorescents in soffits above throw light on the bookshelves and provide ambient lighting for the whole room.

the nozzle can be compared to ambient lighting—it washes gently over a large area. The narrow, focused position of the nozzle can be likened to task lighting. Ambient lighting provides the general lighting in your workplace, whereas task lighting is usually focused on work surfaces, with higher levels of illumination.

In home workplaces, a common form of ambient lighting is recessed lighting. Here, fixtures are inserted within the ceiling, flush to the outer plane. The light source is typically incandescent, with a dimmer control. It's generally not a good idea to use this kind of light for work-surface illumination, because the light source is too far from the surface and it tends to throw shadows, which accelerate eye fatigue.

▲What's the attraction of working at home? If this is the view from your workplace window, it sure beats staring at a wall divider at corporate HQ.

▲ Everything but the chair. With a great view, well-planned lighting, articulated trays for telephone and keyboard, an adjustable monitor arm, and a cantilevered desk to maximize knee room, this corner work space exemplifies a comfortable and healthy environment.

The two most common forms of task lighting are strip fluorescent and halogen lamps with flexible arms. Strip lighting is great when you have a long work surface against a wall, with bookshelves above. By mounting continuous strip lighting under the lowest shelf, you evenly illuminate the surface. The light source should be at least 16 in. above the work surface, and a baffle or valance should be provided so that the light source won't be directly visible. The light tubes can be ordered for a cool or warm light dispersion, depending upon your preference. Another nice feature of this system is that it's out of the way and doesn't take up valuable workstation surface.

Halogen task lamps are becoming increasingly popular because they generate intense light from a small point source and are less obtrusive. If they are mounted on articulating arms, you can locate the source close to the work at hand, or move it out of the way when it's not needed.

## Seating and Ergonomic Tools

Although the focus of this book is on the built home workplace environment, it wouldn't be complete without at least some passing remarks on seating and other ergonomic tools as they relate to computer workstations. If you spend any serious time at a computer, you should have a good task chair—with adjustable height, arms, and lumbar support. Also, your monitor should be positioned properly, and you should have a height-adjustable keyboard tray (see the sidebar below). These features are essential for the long-term health of your eyes, spine, neck, and wrists.

## Design a Place for Who You Are

Being able to design your own workplace is at once the greatest advantage of working at home and the greatest challenge. Working at home offers you the opportunity to personalize your environment in a way that would be impossible in the traditional

▲ No work space is complete if it doesn't express and reflect the personality of the occupant. The owner of this dedicated workplace personalized the room with a large oil painting behind the desk and items of special significance on and around the workstation.

### Healthy Keyboarding

As a rule, the more positioning flexibility you can design into a workstation, especially a computer workstation, the more user-friendly it will be. Start with a standard work surface, set about 30 in. off the floor, then add ergonomic tools that allow positioning flexibility. Position the top of the monitor at or below eye level and 18 in. to 24 in. away. An adjustable chair will help position you at the right height relative to the monitor.

An adjustable keyboard tray is an indispensable piece of equipment. The keyboard tray should be able to slide out from below the surface and to be raised and lowered. It's also preferable to have a separate mouse tray with similar adjusting features.

workplace. The environment you create, yours to organize and decorate as you wish, should be a reflection of your personality. The more successful you are in translating the space that you choose into a place for who you are, the more successful your home workplace will be. You'll find that it becomes a place you gravitate toward, rather than just go to.

A workplace in a walkout basement doesn't have to be dark and dreary. The owner has taken the time to personalize this alcove work space with brightly finished built-in cabinets and a whimsical tree support under the desktop. The tree motif continues in the branch handles of the doors and drawers.

People choose to work at home not just to save on gasoline, but, more important, because it allows them to be something they cannot be in a corporate office. Without a distinctive personality, a home workplace might just as well be anybody's. By personalizing your space, you take ownership. In each of the chapters that follow, you'll find stories that highlight how different people have made their home workplaces unique, how they've created a place that's just right for who they are.

In this opening chapter, I've covered the basics of home workplace design in every

An aficionado of the Arts and Crafts style replicated period details and furnishings in this shared sitting room and workplace. The workstation isn't exactly high tech, but it's certainly in keeping with the style of the room.

▲ Inca tapestries and ancient artifacts line the curved walls of an anthropologist's home work space, dwarfing the computer equipment below.

circumstance I've encountered or could imagine. My hope is that you'll avoid some of the pitfalls that many people make when they enter into this relatively new way of living and working. Now let's look at some specific examples of home workplaces. I've chosen them because no matter how minuscule or grand, how simple or complex, they demonstrate the *balance, organization,* and *spirit* that are the three hallmarks of a well-planned home work space. If you follow the basic planning and design advice I've given in this chapter, I'm certain that your new home workplace will soon join their ranks.

# 2

# Shared Spaces

► A home workplace in a guest bedroom that's used for visitors just a couple of times a year makes good use of otherwise wasted space. This simple but well-appointed workstation sits below the gable-end window of an upstairs bedroom with a view out to the pines.

F or many people, working at home begins as an experiment with which they have no prior experience. It may start out as a one- or two-day-a-week telecommuting arrangement, or it may coincide with the start of a new home-based business or career. If you're just setting out on the road to working at home, you're understandably cautious about allocating money and space. If you have an apartment or a house and family, you might not have much space to spare. A logical approach, therefore, is to look for a place in the home that can serve double duty—a room or area that can be shared for domestic use *and* for business use.

The most common candidates for shared use are bedrooms, kitchens, and what I call gathering rooms—

◄ A large, open room in a New York City apartment does double duty as workplace and dining area for its interior-designer owner. The main workstation is along the back wall, separated from the conference/layout table in the foreground by a floor-to-ceiling glass-panel screen. As necessary, the table reverts to its original function as a dining table.

◀All work and no pool can make for a dull life. This small, somewhat masculine room, with convenient double French doors opening to the rear yard, has all the right stuff for a shared den and workplace.

that is, living rooms, dining rooms, family rooms, sitting rooms, and dens. If you don't expect visitors and have no employees, a shared space may be a workable option. But you'll have to plan carefully for privacy while you work—and for protection of your work area when it's not in use.

Not all rooms can comfortably serve double functions. A lot will depend on how much time you expect to work at home, the specific room you choose, and your family situation. A large room with an open corner might seem like the perfect candidate for a small office, but if the other end of the room is an entertainment center and you have three kids in the house, you probably won't get a lot of work done. On the other hand, if you live alone, a shared-space workplace may be all that you ever need. ■

## Pick Your Spot

If you're lucky enough to have a choice of rooms in which to set up a work space, consider what you will be competing against in each one. A guest bedroom typically remains empty much of the time, whereas a kitchen, family room, or living room promises to be busy—and noisy—on a regular basis. Bedrooms are typically unused for much of the day, but not everyone feels comfortable sleeping next to their work.

# Negotiating Privacy, Setting Boundaries

One of the cardinal rules of working at home is to keep your job separate from your home life. However, when your only option is to establish your work space in an active living area of the house, that's easier said than done. It will be necessary for you and your family to make some compromises. Let's look at an example to see how it might work.

You're considering your den as a potential location for a home workplace. You've already concluded that there's a little extra room in there, and you'll be able to outfit it with a workstation and some storage without having to move the giant-screen TV out of the way. You can already envision

▼ A workstation in a family/dining room works fine for occasional use, but it's likely to be off-limits for business at mealtimes and when the kids are home.

yourself starting your workday peacefully, while you savor that first cup of freshly brewed coffee.

But before you get ahead of yourself, have you thought about what happens when the kids come home from school and want to watch their favorite TV show? Who uses the room in the evening and on the weekend? The privacy and sanctity of your new home workplace can quickly become mired in a territorial tug-of-war.

Privacy in a shared space is better achieved by negotiation than by conflict. Family members will resent the loss of space if they don't feel they're getting something in return. These potential problems must be settled before you pick your spot. As a solution to the shared den work space, buying a small portable TV for use in another room might be a feasible compromise. You'll also need to come to some agreement with your family as to how and when the shared space is used for living or for working. For instance, it might be agreed upon that the den is off-limits to family until a certain time, say, after dinner.

Negotiating the privacy hurdle is just one aspect of working in a shared space. You'll also need to find a way of setting physical boundaries and protecting your work territory. The boundary can be a permanent architectural feature—such as a half-height wall or a built-in bookcase—but it doesn't

▲One of the keys to designing a successful shared work space is to create a boundary between the work area and the living area. Here, a low, built-in storage unit separates the two without blocking the view or the light.

◄In spaces that do double duty, a mobile storage bin can be pressed into service as a room divider. This sturdy shelving unit has been fitted with industrial locking-wheel casters and can be turned at 90 degrees to cordon off the workstation from the larger open space.

◄An unusual custom-designed, curvilinear wood screen pivots around a corner column. The screen alternately exposes or conceals a kitchen in this swing space, which can be quickly converted from living to office/meeting area. The more private bedroom spaces are located above, connected by the stair.

▲A counter built into a 7-ft. by 15-ft. screen provides an eating place for one or two people.

have to be. Equally effective are arrangements of furniture or storage units, a freestanding privacy screen, or even a beaded curtain or a few well-positioned houseplants. The objective is not so much to wall yourself off in a corner of the room but to make it clear to family members that this is where you work. The barrier implies "leave things alone here."

Protection for your work territory might be accomplished by cabinetry, or by obtaining a self-contained, custom-built or store-bought home-office unit that can be closed when not in use. Protection accomplishes a number of things. First and foremost, it shows respect for those who share

▲▲ A hive-like reading cocoon offers the ultimate in privacy in a shared space. The shelves are double-loaded, with books on the outside as well as in, which has the added benefit of significant acoustic insulation.

your living space. An in-use workplace shouldn't stare open-faced at family members or dinner guests after work hours. Even if you live alone, it helps to be able to close off the work area when the space reverts to domestic use so you can forget about work for a few hours. Protection also prevents the inevitable territorial groping that takes place at the borders (in either direction). A lack of clear demarcation invites disorder.

An added benefit of setting up boundaries and protection in a shared space is that it will force you to stay organized. You'll be obliged to put stuff back where it belongs when you end a work session. Valuable equipment and supplies can also be physically protected—from assaults by a frisky pup or a roving toddler.

## Sound Control

You can achieve privacy only if you control sound. In shared or niche spaces, some of that control has to be negotiated with the people you live with—they'll have to respect your need to work in an undisturbed environment. But there are also physical (and portable) ways to control sound in a shared space.

One option is to use a 6-ft.-high sound-absorbent screen, which not only reduces the noise level but also provides a visual and territorial barrier for your workstation. If you'd rather retain the visual connection with the rest of the room, consider using a screen with transparent panels, which will still provide some sound reduction. Screens can be folded and put in a corner when not in use. A simple solution such as installing carpeting in the room where you work can also keep the noise level down.

Even in dedicated work spaces, sound transmission into the room can be distracting. When constructing a new workplace in a basement, attic, or garage, it's a good idea to install insulation in walls, floors, and ceilings that are adjacent to living space. This is easy and relatively inexpensive if done before the exposed framing is covered with finishing materials. Insulating the room not only reduces sound transmission, of course, but also makes the room more comfortable to work in.

▼▶In a space where work and domestic life coexist, it's great to be able to hide things away when you switch out of full work mode. Here, a work surface on wheels tucks away neatly into a cabinet, and keyboard and printer can be concealed behind cabinet doors. The custom design also integrates a heating duct within the toe space of the cabinetry.

Now that we've considered the challenges and benefits of working at home in a shared space, let's take a look at a variety of shared workplaces in apartments, lofts, and single-family homes around the United States. As you weigh up the options for your own home workplace, remember to ask yourself the critical control questions (about privacy, protection, and separation) before you decide on a location. ■

# Shared
# Bedrooms

Bedrooms can be a workable choice for a shared home workplace. They are usually unused for most of the day, and since they are designed as private rooms, they often provide necessary quiet and isolation. That's the good news. For many people, however, the oil and water of intimate bedroom and functional work space simply don't mix. Perhaps the biggest downside is that you commit yourself to trying to sleep next to your work, a prospect that many people find unnerving. If you're not living alone, you must also deal with the fact that your partner may want to sleep while you need to work.

▼If the room is large enough, it's less of a challenge to blend a work space into a bedroom environment. Here, the desk and bed are similarly styled, yet the U-shaped workplace arrangement provides a sense of separation.

▼ Low-slung built-in cabinets and a counter along the entire length of this bedroom perimeter wall provide a combination of dresser and work space. The desk area is centered on the window for the benefit of light and view. All furnishings are kept low, with no shelving on the walls. This minimal design approach makes the room feel larger and also makes it easier to maintain order.

▲ The work area in this bedroom is screened behind a low dividing wall, which also serves as a headboard for the bed and as storage for the workstation. Dropped pendant lights over the work area reinforce the separation between the two parts of the room.

## Screening a Workstation in a Shared Bedroom

**Placing a screen between the work zone and the sleep zone provides some visual privacy between the two. It also hides the workstation clutter and screens the view from the entry.**

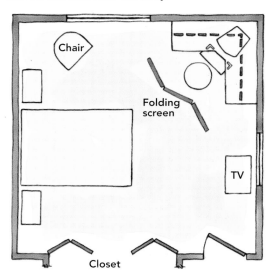

Chair

Folding screen

TV

Closet

If you decide that your bedroom can double as a workplace, screening off the work area can alleviate some of those potential problems. A simple folding screen provides visual privacy between the sleep zone and the work zone—and hides the clutter (see the drawing at left). But the master bedroom is definitely not a place to bring visitors or staff. You'll have to make other arrangements, such as holding meetings in another room of the house or in a remote location.

## Guest Bedrooms

Of all the shared-space arrangements, a workplace in a guest bedroom is one of the better choices. This is a room that is used only occasionally, so privacy and protection are much more attainable than in other parts of the house. However

in arranging the guest room for workplace activities, you should give some thought to the occasions when it will be occupied by guests.

Design arrangements that enclose, hide, or screen the workplace—especially the project station—will make guests feel less like intruders. Papers and files should be stowed and out of sight. And when you have overnight visitors, make arrangements to work in another location.

On the other hand, you don't want your workplace to feel like a bedroom. To this end, give some serious thought to "hiding" the beds. You can do this by putting in a sofa bed, which has the added benefit of providing day sitting space

◄This nicely conceived designer's home work space doubles as guest bedroom. Drawing files serve as the foundation for a spare bed, while the bulk of the work space is built within what was once a closeted area. A tackboard behind the administrative workstation and storage above keep the desk space free. The drawing table project station is placed right at the view. There's even room for a small television, perched on the fortuitously deep windowsill.

►This dramatic small space, in the corner of a converted New York City loft, comfortably combines sleep with work. Floor space under the table is used for two-tiered storage, while a curtain of white Lycra screens off the work space from the adjacent dining area.

in either the guest-room or workplace mode. To capture even more square footage and maintain open space, you might want to install a Murphy bed, which either folds up flat against the wall or is contained in its own wall-unit-like closet cabinet. ■

# At Work in the Treetops

When the owners of this small house on a sloping lot in upstate New York approached architect Dennis Wedlick, their design direction was clear: They wanted to build a home that would cause minimal disruption to the densely wooded landscape. The result was a compact three-story house on a small footprint that made the most of the forest's filtered daylight.

At the top of the house, a writing studio wrapped in windows adjoins the master bedroom. When the studio is in use, closing the sliding doors provides the necessary privacy and separation. When overnight visitors come to stay, the writing studio converts to a guest bedroom. Either way, with 6½-ft.-high double-hung windows spaced tightly together around the outside walls, the light and views are spectacular.

▲ The small footprint and vertical plan saved on foundation and minimized disruption of the site. The studio is on the third floor, with windows facing south and west.

## Third-Floor Shared Space

Writing studio doubles as guest bedroom when pocket doors are closed.

▲ The third-floor studio in working mode. The studio doubles as a guest bedroom.

As a general rule, kitchens don't make particularly good home workplaces because in most houses they are the center of busy family life and traffic. Food preparation, cooking and washing activities, and noise add to the disadvantages. But for those who use the workplace (or the kitchen) sporadically, the arrangement might work just fine. For example, if you're just looking for a space where you can keep up with the workload from your full-time job on

▼ **The little work alcove** in this kitchen is out of the way of the triangle formed by the refrigerator, stove, and sink. In this arrangement, Mom or Dad can catch up with a little paperwork while the kids do their homework at the kitchen island.

▲With matching custom built-in cabinetry, this workplace is well integrated into the kitchen area. The overall space is large enough that the workplace is removed from the kitchen triangle.

evenings and weekends, the kitchen table might be all you ever need. Because you have a full-time work space away from the house, you're not going to need extensive storage or a place to meet clients.

On the other hand, if your home business is kitchen related—if you are a caterer or a pastry chef, for instance—that's a whole different story. You may want a little space for fielding calls and taking orders right in the kitchen. Even so, it's unlikely that this will eliminate your need for a serious administrative station outside the kitchen area. ■

▲If you're going to work in the kitchen, make sure your workstation is away from the cooking and food-prep areas. This light-duty workstation is located at the end of a counter run, separated from the cooking area by floor-to-ceiling cabinets.

▲This end-cap workplace between the kitchen and laundry room is equipped with a computer mounted beneath the counter. Here, it's out of the way of all the things that people like and computers don't—such as liquids and granular substances. Keyboard and mouse slide beneath the counter when not in use, while custom cabinets below harbor the central processing unit (CPU) and other peripherals—protected and out of sight.

◄Sharing space with a laundry may not be everyone's idea of the dream home office, but if the space is there why not use it? Workplaces in utility rooms like this one are becoming increasingly popular, sometimes offered as specialty rooms within new spec homes. They make reasonably efficient workplaces because the sharing is mainly done with equipment and the foot traffic is controllable.

# Shared Gathering Rooms

Living rooms, family rooms, and dens are often chosen for home workplaces because they are typically larger rooms and are therefore more flexible to change. If you live alone, or if you and your spouse are empty-nesters, the sharing will probably be more workable. These rooms are usually in central locations in the house and are subject to noise, disruption, and nearby foot traffic. If you're displacing prior tenants, such as your spouse and kids—even if only for part of the day—consider the consequences carefully before you make your decision to share.

In a shared gathering space, it's especially important to protect the work area by enclosing it somehow—using a screen, a storage unit, or one of the other barriers mentioned earlier in this chapter. This will also make the room more comfortable for everyone when the shared space reverts to its original intended use.

▲ When shoehorning a workstation into a shared space, it's important to match the area with the style of the house and its furnishings. By repeating the molding profiles and observing the shapes of the cabinets in the rest of the room, this computer workstation located in a study alcove was made to fit right into the Prairie-style home.

A home workplace fits comfortably into the corner of a living room with minimal disruption to the space. Office supplies are stored elsewhere, and views to the outside are kept open by keeping furnishings away from the windows. The computer monitor is located in the corner of the room, away from glare.

## Blending In

When setting up shop in a shared space, it's important to respect the domestic character of the room. You want to create a comfortable spot that's devoted to work, but you need to make sure that the primary function of the room dictates the design. After all, you don't want your living room to look like corporate headquarters.

Begin your planning by focusing on the furnishings—on desks, cabinets, and bookcases, which are the most visible components of most home work spaces. Think of your work furnishings as home furniture as well as office equipment. That way, the workstation will blend in with the rest of the room when it reverts to its nonwork function.

In a space that does double duty as a dining room, you don't want to be staring at a filing cabinet over lunch. Doors in this well-planned wall unit have fabric panels and wire mesh to screen office equipment that doesn't store attractively.

As in any shared space, it's important that you are sensitive to the design of the room when you plan your home workplace; it should blend in, not scream out (see the sidebar at left and the photo on the facing page).

▲A little over the top? Maybe. But when you're planning your own home workplace, let it reflect your personality. This beautifully detailed sitting room/workplace does just that. On a practical level, the custom-built racetrack-end desk is supported by a single slender wooden column, which frees up leg room on either side.

▲Lighting in a shared workplace should be low and focused. To avoid dark corners, use a light focused on the work surface rather than overhead or accent lighting. A flexible task lamp or fluorescent strip lighting under a shelf should be all you need.

Sitting rooms fall into the general category of gathering rooms, though quite often they are extra rooms to begin with. As a result, you may be able to use them as workplaces without necessarily depriving others of space. Even though technically shared, they may behave more like dedicated spaces (see chapter 4). Similarly, dining rooms sit unused in many houses for weeks on end, and they can serve as workplaces with only minimal disruption to family life. ■

◄The workstation blends seamlessly into the adobe living room of this renovated, Spanish Colonial-style home—so much so that you barely notice it's there. The workstation is nothing more than a plank of laminated plywood atop a pair of basic storage units. Clearly not designed as a "power" station, it seems perfect for short but leisurely stints of work, interspersed with relaxation in front of the *kiva* fireplace.

▲Inch for inch, a corner workstation can be the most efficient and least disruptive use of shared space. Here, custom-designed shelving holds peripheral computer equipment and also shoots below the desk area to provide additional shelving in what would have been unused space. Thin-profile drawers provide storage below the work surface, which is cantilevered across the corner to maximize knee room.

## Making the Most of a Wall-Mounted Workstation

When space is tight, spread up, not out.

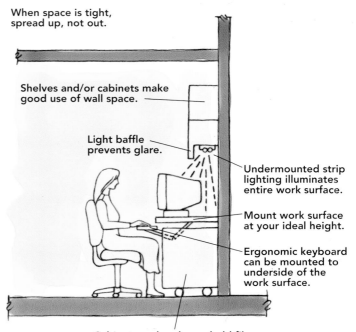

Shelves and/or cabinets make good use of wall space.

Light baffle prevents glare.

Undermounted strip lighting illuminates entire work surface.

Mount work surface at your ideal height.

Ergonomic keyboard can be mounted to underside of the work surface.

Cabinets and end caps hold files and supplies; can be movable.

# One Home, Two Workplaces

If you think it's hard to find room for one work space in your home, try fitting in two. This was just the challenge that Bev and Don faced, though they did have the advantage of building new—and of having full-time jobs outside the home.

Bev and Don both work at the local university. Although they have offices on campus, Bev comments that she "can't get a thing done there" because of continual interruptions. So when they began to plan their new Craftsman-style house in north-

▲Recycled, hand-sorted, split shakes—scrap from a nearby school reroofing project—add character to the Craftsman-style home.

ern California, two workplaces at home were high on the wish list. They didn't want a big house (total square footage is just over 2,000 sq. ft.), so they knew that the work spaces would probably have to do double duty.

The inspiration for Don's work area was an old Charlie Chan movie, in which he'd seen the master detective at work at a big, heavy desk by the fire. Like Charlie, Don had only modest equipment needs (admittedly Chan didn't have a laptop), and he figured there'd be enough room for a

◀The downstairs workplace is tucked into the corner of the living room. Mission-style furnishings help the workstation blend in with the Craftsman detailing of the rest of the room.

## Finding Room for Two Work Spaces

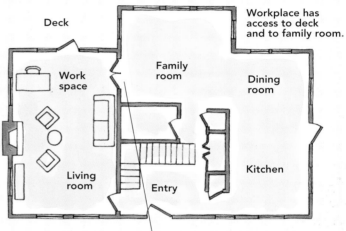

**FIRST FLOOR**

Deck

Workplace has access to deck and to family room.

Work space

Family room

Dining room

Living room

Entry

Kitchen

French doors to family room can be opened when living room reverts to nonwork mode.

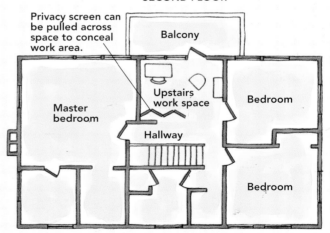

**SECOND FLOOR**

Privacy screen can be pulled across space to conceal work area.

Balcony

Master bedroom

Upstairs work space

Bedroom

Hallway

Bedroom

workstation in the corner of the living room, the largest room in the house. A French door behind the workstation connects to a deck, offering nice views and plenty of light; a cozy family room is just a few steps away.

The choice of location for Bev's workplace wasn't so easy. Initially, the couple were considering a combined guest room and office, but Bev was concerned that the shared arrangement could create potential conflicts of use. At the suggestion of designer/builder Gene Callahan, they decided instead to open a tiny second-floor room to the hall, creating a niche space in the hallway for Bev's workplace. A folding screen can be set up between the workplace and hallway for visual privacy. (There's a photo of the screen in use on p. 13.)

# Storage in Shared Spaces

It's tough to manage all your workplace needs when you're operating in a shared space. You'll probably need to consider moving some things out of the shared space and into other areas of the house. Storage is usually the first thing to go—but there's the problem of keeping it handy. Active storage—things like books, files, and records—need to be readily accessible. Inactive storage—the stuff you don't need every day—can go anywhere in the house. If you think creatively, you'll find there are a number of ways to solve the problem of fitting everything you need for work into your existing home. ■

▼The owner of this living room/workplace found space for extra storage by building shelves over the fireplace and above the windows. The shelves are close to the workstation and accessed by a rolling library ladder, an interesting design element in this light-filled room.

◀Walls make great surfaces for storage, but when windows intrude you may need to set your sights lower. The long shelf below this work surface makes the most of an otherwise wasted space. It's beyond the knee space, so it doesn't prevent the owner from cozying up to the computer.

▲When space is tight, one solution is to move some functions out of the work space and into a hallway. Here, a second-floor landing houses file storage and a copier, freeing up floor area within the workplace (which is behind the door).

▲Inactive storage is out of the way yet accessible. A super-long maple storage unit supported by a structural-steel frame houses 70 aluminum file boxes. The clever design turns storage into a thing of beauty.

# 3

# Niche Spaces

As you look around your home for a suitable place to work, don't be afraid to be a little creative. There's no rule that says you need a whole room for your workplace. Maybe there's a little nook or an alcove within a larger room you can lay claim to or a small closet you can convert to a work area to suit your needs. Perhaps there's a nesting space in an unused area below a stair, along a hallway, or off the beaten path in a loft. I call these postage-stamp pieces of real-estate "niche spaces."

You might think that a tiny niche space would be less desirable than a more expansive shared space, but it's not always about size. A space that has physical boundaries—a closet door, a sliding screen, a partition—provides a degree of privacy,

►Contrasting colors, light woods, and a dropped ceiling turn an ordinary corner into a workplace of special interest. Alcove shelving screens clutter from the space at large. The room doubles as an extra bedroom when guests stay over.

◄An empty, out-of-the-way corner can serve as a perfect spot for a portable office. The owner of this Maine cottage takes advantage of an upstairs hallway to set up a temporary workstation, with great views outside and to the great room below.

protection, and separation that's missing in a larger, open shared space. As we saw in chapter 1, it's all about control.

If you can't fit all your workplace needs into the little piece of space that's available, there's always the option of using other space within your home for the overflow. Inactive storage could be elsewhere or in some adjacent space—a copying machine might find a home nestled in a space nearby, for example. In this chapter, we'll look at various types of niche work spaces up close and examine some of the creative solutions that their owners have come up with. ▪

◄The owner—who is also the designer—uses this warm, stylized nook to meet with clients and to lay out presentation materials on the double-wide desk.

# Nooks and Alcoves within Larger Rooms

A nook, or an alcove, within a larger common area is subject to the same privacy issues we talked about in chapter 2. Even so, a nook offers you more protection than a workplace in a shared space because it has physical definition and is distinct from the surrounding living space. Once a workplace is established within it, the space is more clearly your territory. There may also be the possibility of closing off the niche with sliding doors or placing a screen in front of it. This will provide your workplace and its contents a degree of protection (and maybe even a little privacy) not afforded in openly shared space. ■

▼This alcove work space is set apart from the rest of the room by an impressive archway with bookshelves on either side, clearly indicating that this is a separate space. The partition wall is used for overflow storage on the non-work side.

▲In situations where more privacy is desired, sliding doors can be used to close off a work space from the connecting room.

▲Getting enough natural light into a niche can be a problem, but this second-floor work space presents an effective solution—even without windows. The work space overlooks the living room through a large opening that borrows light from windows on the opposite wall. The hole in the ceiling draws additional natural light from an atrium on the floor above.

## Do You Have Enough Space?

If you're thinking of working in a tight niche, don't forget the space you'll need around your equipment. For example, copy machines have paper-feed trays on the side that take up space, and you'll need additional room to remove them. You may need an additional surface or bin to catch the paper that rolls out of your fax machine. Remember, also, that most office equipment produces heat that is ventilated from the sides and top. If you jam equipment into tight spots and prevent air circulation, you can damage the equipment.

◀ This narrow alcove has just enough space for a musician's recording equipment, with a little room left over for a tiny computer station along the back wall. An unusual hanging light and artfully framed black-and-white photos against the pastel walls create a highly personalized work space in what might otherwise have been a dark corner of the house.

◀▲ If you're going to set up a workplace in the kitchen, the ideal is to cordon off a niche. This office nook is separated from the galley kitchen by a perforated wood screen and by a step up (above). The extra step places the owner at a comfortable level to enjoy the view out to the side yard. Another window over the desk provides a view to the dining room and living room (left).

▶This little cubbyhole, equipped with computer, fax, and phone, is well positioned relative to the front entry of the house. The owner can receive overnight deliveries and greet visitors without having them come into the more private parts of the house. A half-wall provides a partial barrier between entry and workplace and offers storage for active files and records.

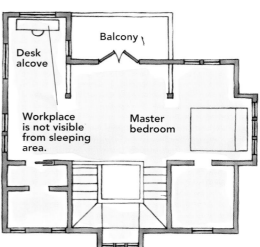

◀A workplace alcove in a bedroom is most effective if it is out of view of the sleeping area.

◀ Built-ins wrap around this odd-angled niche, creating a workplace that's a model of efficiency with everything within easy reach. Tackboard surfaces and carpeting are color-matched and custom-fit into the irregular shape.

▶ Dividing a room with shelves to form an intimate book nook adds a significant amount of storage space.

# Mother's Little Cupboard

Architect Carol Kurth designed this nifty niche workplace for a work-at-home mother as part of the larger renovation of a 1980s home north of New York City.

The new office, in what was a laundry room (now relocated), is strategically positioned near the kitchen and on the same level as the kids' bedrooms. Glass pocket doors at the entry can be closed for sound control, but Mom still has a visual connection and is only steps away from key family

▲Open cubbies and shoebox cubbies hold supplies and are readily accessible from the workstation.

◀Beautifully organized custom cabinetry along one wall is the key to making this tiny space highly habitable—and highly functional.

spaces. At the other end of the niche, a window overlooks the front entry so she can watch for the kids coming home from school and also keep an eye out for overnight business deliveries.

One of the more interesting aspects of this workplace, designed with a Craftsman-style influence, is the carefully planned and beautifully constructed cabinetry. Drawers, cabinets, and cubbies are carefully sized and located to contain the very specific requirements of the user. The choice of natural cherry for the cabinets, offset against the natural oak floor, gives what could otherwise be a corporate office a warm, homey feel.

## A Niche off the Entry

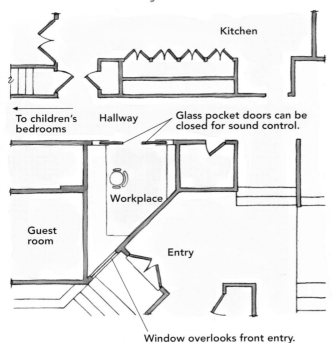

Kitchen

To children's bedrooms

Hallway

Glass pocket doors can be closed for sound control.

Workplace

Guest room

Entry

Window overlooks front entry.

▲To the left of the knee space, a narrow cabinet houses the computer tower, a piece of equipment that might otherwise be in the way.

# A Flexible Niche Takes Center Stage

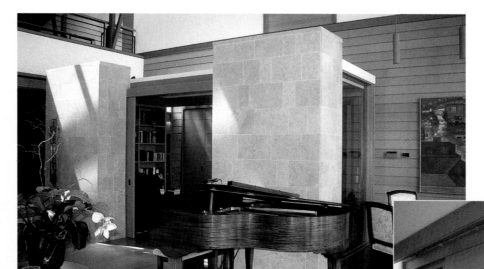

◀▼Sliding doors between the workplace and the main living area can be closed for privacy. As the sliding doors are closed, additional bookshelves are revealed on the workplace side.

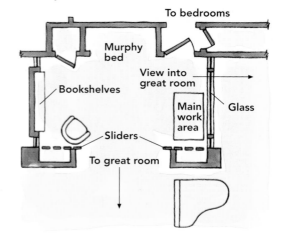

The owner of this contemporary residence, designed by architect George Suyama, placed his home workplace smack-dab in the middle of things. Almost like a kiosk, it sits at the main crossroads of interior circulation, with sliders that open wide onto a soaring, 30-ft.-high living area and a swinging door that leads to the more private bedroom wing. A glass wall provides a view into the great room so that when doors are closed, there's a visual connection to the larger living space.

What's most interesting about this workplace arrangement is its flexibility. If the owner has guests, he can open the sliders and use the little room as an intimate sitting area. Should he choose privacy, he simply closes the sliders and has a secondary exit through the bedroom suite. The office also converts to a guest room, complete with a Murphy bed well hidden behind elegant sliding doors, for when the grandkids come to stay.

## Workplace Central

To bedrooms

Murphy bed

View into great room

Bookshelves

Main work area

Glass

Sliders

To great room

Remove the closet pole and hat shelf from a standard 24-in.-deep closet, add a long work surface with cabinets below and shelves above, and you've got a compact work space that can be closed off when not in use. Of course, you'll have to find a home for all the stuff that was stored in the closet before, but setting up an office in a shared or a niche space almost always involves trade-offs.

Wide-faced closets aren't the only candidates for conversion to office space. Another option, and one that typically gives you a bit more room, is a walk-in closet. In either case, you'll have to carefully analyze lighting, power, and ventilation needs, all of which may be new to the space. Because most closets are windowless, the introduction of artificial light is very important. Work-

▲ How much space do you really need? A transformed closet offers many benefits: It is compact and self-contained, with lots of wall space for storage, and it can be easily hidden behind closed doors. Here, a printer on a rolling cart pulls out when the work space is in use and tucks back into the under-counter knee space when the chair is pulled away and the doors are closed.

◀ A cleverly concealed wall of closets in a Boston loft features a complete home office on the right and a library of books (behind closed doors) on the left. When both closets are closed, the room returns to its dedicated use as living space.

surface space is often at a premium, so lighting that takes up little or no space (such as under-shelf strip fluorescents) is ideal. If the closet is large enough to work inside, you'll have to consider air-exchange requirements. In any event, a closet will have to be wired for electricity and communications.

## Wide-Faced Closets

Wide-faced closets are usually 2 ft. deep and can be anywhere from 5 ft. to 10 ft. wide. The doors are typically sliders, which should be replaced, or double bifold doors, which can part away from the work area and enclose it when it's not in use. Bifold doors can open up the whole length of the closet to reveal a long work surface, which might be supported below with storage cabinets. Above the work surface, you can introduce shelving or upper cabinets.

▲ Every inch counts in a 24-in. closet. Cabinets below support the work surface, a top drawer is cleverly retrofit to double as a mouse tray, and an adjustable keyboard tray slides away when not in use. A small, portable fan between the monitor and the printer circulates air.

An existing closet is bumped out into the living space to provide the necessary depth for a fully functioning home work space. When the office is in shutdown mode, you'd never know it exists. Even with the sliding doors open, the space is sensitive to the design of the larger room. Built-in shelving to either side of the closet is used for overflow storage and equipment.

## Light in the Closet

If you have a computer station in the closet, you'll want to be careful not to introduce light that could cause veiling reflections—light rays that bounce off a reflective surface (in this case the monitor) and ricochet into your eyes, causing eyestrain and fatigue. One way to control veiling reflections from an artificial light source is to use a flexible-arm task light, with a shade that obscures the light source.

You can then mount fluorescent lighting to the underside of the shelving or cabinets, which will give you bright and even illumination along your entire work surface. The nice part about this arrangement is that the workplace is out of sight when the doors are closed—there's your control—and it looks good, too.

◄One way to create work space in your home is to open up a small room to a larger room. It might be a powder room, a walk-in closet that's no longer in use, or, as in this case, a converted bar. The niche space serves as a combined project and administration station, while the rest of the room is a comfortable seating area for meeting with clients.

## From Closet to Work Space

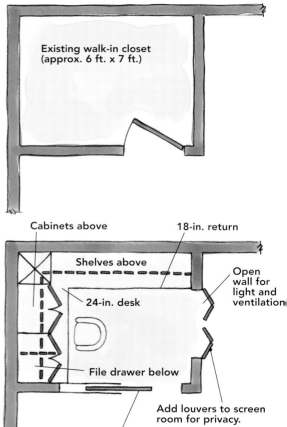

Existing walk-in closet
(approx. 6 ft. x 7 ft.)

Cabinets above                    18-in. return

Shelves above

Open
wall for
light and
ventilation

24-in. desk

File drawer below

Add louvers to screen
room for privacy.

Pocket door slides
out of the way.

## Walk-In Closets

To turn a walk-in closet into a comfortable work environment you'll have to open it up to allow light and air to come in. Chances are that the open door itself won't provide enough light or circulation. You might want to consider opening a portion of the wall, preferably within view of a window (but check with an architect or structural engineer first). Small, closed spaces such as this build up heat quite readily. A through-the-wall fan strategically placed may be enough to transfer air from the larger room into the closet. ■

▲▶Originally conceived as a walk-in closet for the adjoining master bedroom, this space now does double duty as a work space. A large layout table in the center of the closet serves as the project station, with shelves behind sized to fit the supplies. On the opposite wall, the computer station is supported by file cabinets and framed by counter-to-ceiling shelving. No space is wasted (and there's still room to store clothes).

# Hallways and Stairwells

Hallways, landings, and spaces under a stair are naturals for workplace niches because you don't normally have to bounce anyone out of occupancy—they're free real estate. But not just any hallway will do. It needs to be wide enough to accommodate the space necessary for the intended workplace use while still maintaining what architects call circulation—a pathway for the comers and goers to adjacent rooms. Depending on the width of the hallway, you might be able to use one or both sides (see the drawing on the facing page).

Unless you live alone, a workplace on a path of circulation won't work well without cooperation from the other occupants of your home. For example, a workplace in a hallway may be perfectly usable during the day, but when the kids get home, what was a peaceful sanctuary may seem as busy as Grand Central Station. For this setup to work, you'll have to come to some agreement that at certain times of the day, the hallway (and even the rooms that abut it) are quiet zones or even off-limits. ▄

▲▶ The second-floor hallway of a San Francisco Victorian is wide enough for two computer stations and a fax/copy station on the opposite wall. The cherry cabinetry blends in seamlessly with the house's period trim.

## How Wide Is Wide Enough?

These are the minimum pass-through widths for hallways and alcoves.

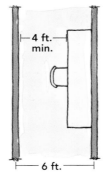

**SINGLE-LOADED HALLWAY PASSAGE**

4 ft. min.

6 ft.

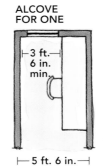

**ALCOVE FOR ONE**

3 ft. 6 in. min.

5 ft. 6 in.

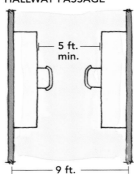

**DOUBLE-LOADED HALLWAY PASSAGE**

5 ft. min.

9 ft.

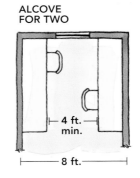

**ALCOVE FOR TWO**

4 ft. min.

8 ft.

▲White trim, pale yellow walls, and natural light from a window to the left transform a short passageway between bedrooms into an open and cheery workplace. Doors can be closed for privacy as needed.

▶Simple but effective. A deep-set alcove in an upstairs hallway is just big enough for a computer workstation, with a built-in desk and cabinet storage above. When not in use, the chair can be tucked in all the way so it's out of the path of circulation.

# Wide Enough for Two

plenty of room for record storage below and shelving above. Custom built-in furnishings, natural-wood flooring and window trim add to the character and warmth of the workplace. All the artificial lighting is either recessed or built into the cabinetry, which reduces the clutter that comes with desk lamps, sconces, or hanging fixtures. The remaining floor width allows for ample passage to the occasionally used guest bedroom.

The owners of this vacation retreat—an architect and an interior designer—wanted a place to work as well as play. They designed a second-floor connecting hallway with a "bump-out" in the front wall that gave them the necessary width to load both sides with everything they needed for a spacious office for two.

The window side with the view is the natural spot for the computer and project workstations. The opposite side of the aisle provides ample counter space, with

▲ Adding a well-lit "bump out" to a second-floor hallway provides all the room needed for a drafting table and computer workstation, with a run of cabinets and shelves across the aisle.

## Office in a Bump-Out

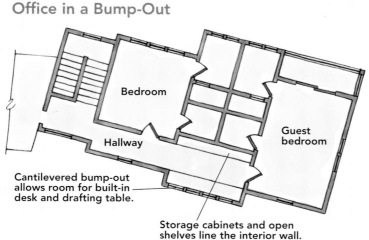

Bedroom

Hallway

Guest bedroom

Cantilevered bump-out allows room for built-in desk and drafting table.

Storage cabinets and open shelves line the interior wall.

◀A midlevel landing between the two legs of a double-back stair provides just enough room for an elegant built-in work station in space that might otherwise go unused. Strip fluorescent lighting along the length of the first shelf above casts strong, even lighting on the work surface, while the large picture window brings the outdoors right into the work space.

## An Office under the Stair

**Open storage for books**

**Tackboard behind for notes**

**Strip fluorescent behind baffle**

**Open cubbies**

**File drawer on wheels can be pulled out as side table.**

**36-in.-wide knee space (min.)**

**Access door to storage below**

If you need to remove a wall to convert space under a stair into a workplace, structural issues may come into play. Make sure to consult an architect or engineer before you get out the saw.

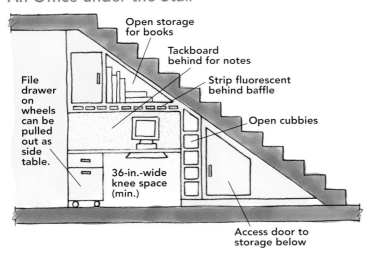

▲The open space below this stair has been reclaimed for storage for the adjoining home workplace. A small round table nearby is used as overflow desk space or for meetings.

# Lofts

We've already established that a niche space is preferable to an open workplace in shared space because it has physical boundaries. If you're fortunate enough to find a niche that's off the beaten path from the main living area, such as in a loft, it will provide you with an even greater degree of privacy.

Lofts make good candidates for workplaces because they are separated from the living space, often with a view down onto it. If access to the loft stair is near an entry, you can greet occasional business visitors, who can be escorted directly to the loft without having to pass through the rest of the house.

▲ This second-floor loft is perfectly situated for a small workplace. A stair directly off the front entry offers separation from the public areas of the house, with views both down into the foyer and to the outside through a pair of double-hung windows. Closet space at the entry can be used for overflow workplace storage.

◄ A compact loft workplace doubles as a bunk/seating area as necessary; space below the bunk is used for storage and books. The view from the workstation is dramatic, and the nautical theme and blue color scheme add to the personal charm of the space.

▲ This angular mezzanine space was pressed into service as a workplace by custom designing a desk whose shape matches the angles of the perimeter railing. Built-in bookcases conserve on valuable floor space.

▲ The owners of this Connecticut home found space for a workplace by turning one room into two. The upper part of the cathedral-ceilinged living room was converted into a studio, with a curved cutout and railing connecting the two rooms. The windows in the gable-end wall were not changed, allowing light to flood into both rooms. Built-in storage and a new row of small windows make the most of the low kneewall space in the studio.

One word of caution: The upper levels of most homes are usually the warmest in the house. Heat will be increased by people, lighting, and electrical equipment (and it usually takes a little more work to run new services to an upper level). You might consider adding an operable skylight to your loft for ventilation. ■

# Office Aloft

One of the big advantages of using a loft for a home workplace is that it is physically separated from the main living area without necessarily being visually detached. This well-designed loft workplace in a 1,200-sq.-ft. home in North Carolina overlooks the living and dining areas on two sides, yet from below you would hardly know it was there.

The floor plan of this house also works extremely well for receiving business visitors to the loft workplace (see the drawing below). Stairs to the loft are immediately to the right of the entry so visitors don't have to pass through the living area. A ground-floor guest bedroom shares a bath at the entry, which can also be used as the visitors' rest room. The living room to the left of the stair can be used as a client meeting space.

## Second-Floor Loft

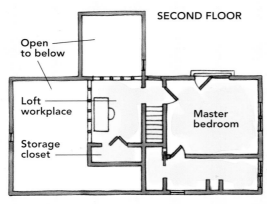

**SECOND FLOOR**

Open to below

Loft workplace

Storage closet

Master bedroom

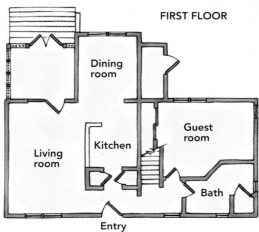

**FIRST FLOOR**

Dining room

Living room

Kitchen

Guest room

Bath

Entry

▲The second-floor loft workplace is accessed by a stair directly from the front entry (visible at rear). Railings on two sides partially screen the workplace from below.

▲ ▶ This work alcove tucked under a steeply
pitched roof at the end of a second-floor balcony is removed from the main living area yet
not totally remote. Stand up at the workstation
and there's a commanding view of the living
area below. Sit down and you can focus on work
(and the view out to the bay beyond). The
exposed chimney helps to anchor and define
the corner of the workplace.

# Dedicated to Work

# 4

I you have a spare room in your house that you can dedicate for use as a home workplace, you're taking a major step up. In there, you'll enjoy privacy and protection merely by shutting the door—and the space can be redefined to suit your particular work needs without the worry of intruding upon living space.

A redefined room such as a bedroom, dining area, or den is cost-effective in comparison with some of the other alternatives. By and large, you need to do the least amount of work to prepare the space for workplace use because it's already conditioned for living. Areas in the home that haven't been previously used for living (such as attics and basements) or rooms that haven't been weatherized (such as sunrooms and porches) will most

►Custom woodwork transforms this spare room in a high-rise apartment into a cool, minimalist home workplace that also doubles as a meeting area. Heating and air conditioning are integrated into the cabinetry. Sleek, floor-to-ceiling closets keep storage out of sight.

◄A grand Palladian window, soaring interior roof planes, custom woodwork, and eye-catching columns enhance the drama of this second-floor workplace over a three-bay garage. There's no mistaking that this is a space dedicated to work.

likely require some general construction just to make them habitable. In addition, construction requirements—such as power runs, lighting, and perhaps built-in cabinets or shelving—will also have to be satisfied. That said, some of the best home workplaces around can be found in what was previously an uninsulated, cobweb-covered attic or an underutilized screened-in porch.

If you have the luxury of starting from scratch, there's no better way to develop a home workplace than to incorporate one into a new house. This gives you the opportunity to accommodate all your needs in a custom-built space. For some people, a home-based workplace is so important that they choose to design their house around it. Some higher-end custom-built homes are now being designed to include dedicated home workplaces

▲When the weather's right, an accessible roof becomes an extension of the owner's loft workplace. With just a chair and a laptop, she can take care of business and enjoy the night air and city skyline.

that rival the finest executive suites in the corporate workplace. We'll look at a couple of these at the end of the chapter, but first let's take a tour of some dedicated workplaces that have been converted from existing rooms in the house. ▪

# Bedrooms, Dens, and Other Redefined Rooms

The big advantage of using a whole room for a workplace is that it can be closed off, thereby offering the privacy and protection that are often lacking in a shared space or a niche space. However, some rooms are more private than others. While a seldom-used dining room or den may seem like an appealing location to open up shop, these rooms are usually near the center of family activity. Even if you can close yourself off behind a door, noise and traffic may make this location impractical. A converted bedroom or spare room on the second floor may be a better option.

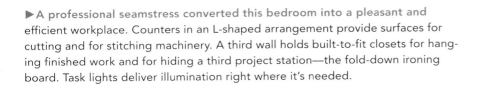

▲A flat door across a pair of sawhorses in front of a wide sliding window was all it took to transform this spare room into a home workplace where a photographer can take care of business.

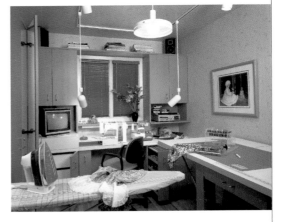

▶A professional seamstress converted this bedroom into a pleasant and efficient workplace. Counters in an L-shaped arrangement provide surfaces for cutting and for stitching machinery. A third wall holds built-to-fit closets for hanging finished work and for hiding a third project station—the fold-down ironing board. Task lights deliver illumination right where it's needed.

A workplace in a converted bedroom takes advantage of built-in perimeter cabinetry, which provides an extended work surface and maintains open floor space in the center of the room. The cabinetry design integrates a metal lateral file cabinet and a computer's central processing unit (CPU). An existing alcove is put to good use by building in a handsome matching storage cabinet. Surface-mounted low-voltage spots—with wiring snaked above the finished ceiling—provide adjustable room light.

## Need More Power?

The electrical power required to run a home workplace, even a small one, is likely to be different and more intense than what's normally available in a residential space such as a family room or a bedroom. For one thing, there never seem to be enough outlets. Depending on the equipment you're running, you also may require one or more additional circuits. For a small office with two computers, printer, fax, and telephone, a single circuit should suffice, but add an air conditioner or a heater, and you'll need a separate circuit.

If you have any doubts about the ability of your work space to carry the additional power load you'll demand from it, consult a licensed electrician. Overloading electrical circuits is not only hazardous to your equipment but can also cause a fire.

Beyond issues of privacy, you'll also have to evaluate whether the room you're thinking of using meets all the needs we identified in chapter 1. Specifically, is the room big enough for the work you plan to do there? Is there adequate storage or space to add cabinets, shelves, and built-ins? How about your energy needs? Is the lighting adequate?

Because this is a room that's dedicated to work—nothing else happens here—you'll have more flexibility in choosing a spot for your workstation than you would in a niche or shared space. As you consider how best to use the space, don't forget the fourth basic step in successful workplace

▼Using standard kitchen cabinets is a cheaper way to go than custom-built. Counters over floor cabinets are usually 36 in. high, so dropped sections in this redefined spare room had to be fabricated for the desk surfaces, which are typically 29 in. or 30 in. high. The overhanging counter at the administrative station provides a pull-up meeting area for two or three people.

▲A custom workstation is typically the best fit for an odd-shaped room. Here, a corner desk makes maximum use of the space available with storage cabinets concentrated at one end, which allows the user plenty of knee room. The cubby areas at the back of the work surface finish out just at the sill of the window. Matching the finish to the existing trim pulls the whole room together.

planning: "Create a comfortable and healthy environment" (see p. 9). Think about lighting, views, and comfortable seating and ergonomic tools. If your budget allows, a custom workstation will make the most of the area and enhance its appearance. It will also give you the benefit of designing to your own personal needs and work requirements. ■

# From Bedroom to Writing Studio

Judy is an English and creative writing teacher who wanted a quiet place at home where she could grade papers and write poetry. She and her husband, Alan, who is a remodeler, collaborated to produce this beautifully detailed home workplace within what was previously a rear bedroom (and before that a long, narrow screened porch).

The first task was to identify Judy's work needs in fine detail. In Alan's words, "Judy and I laid out the desk details together. She sat at her old desk, and we arranged things within reach and tried to keep the most frequently used items close to the seating position. The computer is centered, with the phone and answering machine on the left to keep her right hand free to write. The tape player and the CD player are left of the phone," with pigeon-

▲ Pivoted awning windows above the workplace fill the room with light and let in some air. The arched opening between the writing room and adjoining bedroom is shaped like a wave or a shell, reflecting the owner's love of the sea.

◄ The added entry door and bump-out bay window turned this small rear bedroom into a wonderful writing studio, with an expanded connection to a sitting area and outdoor garden. The brackets that support the bay were bandsawn to resemble the flowers of the overhanging trumpet vine.

◄The workstation was meticulously planned so there's a place for everything—even the cubbies are sized so that there's no wasted space. The left end of the L-shaped work surface is gracefully curved back toward the doorway opening to allow comfortable passage in and out of the room.

▼There's an old adage that if you want to test the mettle of a cabinetmaker, look underneath. Here, the work surface load is carried into the wall via custom-shaped 4x6s, which eliminate the need for legs. The wall behind is outfitted with a wire chase. The cable you see is for the computer keyboard, which rests on a movable tray.

holes for all the various storage items that Judy needs close at hand.

Once he'd determined Judy's specific requirements, Alan was able to size the workstation—both vertically and horizontally—fitting it neatly into the bay area niche he planned. The height of the window ledge was based on the height of the largest item on the work surface, which is the computer monitor. The glass area above wraps around the workstation and expands the space visually, while bathing it in natural light. Recessed lighting in the step-paneled ceiling above provides supplemental task light around and at the work surface.

Alan likens the detailing of the room interior to the "warmth and intimacy of a

ship's cabin," which is only fitting given Judy's love of the sea and all things nautical. His generous use of finely crafted wood carries through the rear door of the workplace and into the garden. The bay window detailing, doorsteps, bench, and wood deck work together to make the garden area feel like a seamless extension of the enclosed workplace.

▲ Family rooms and dens are good candidates for conversion to home workplaces because they are usually among the larger rooms in the house and they sometimes have a separate entrance. This fully functional workplace, with stations for computer, project, and administrative work, makes it on both counts. The window seat softens the room and provides a cozy spot to take a break from work.

◀Dining rooms are often underutilized. This one was converted to a research room and library, with a dramatic color scheme and wall-to-wall, thin-line shelving. The shade at the window provides privacy without blocking natural light. Low-voltage spots mounted on ceiling tracks can be adjusted for general room lighting and for task lighting at the main table.

▶Bookshelves and work surface are integrated in this writer's study. The shelf immediately behind the desk stores readily accessible supplies, while the top surface of the roll-out taboret frees up a little desk space. An inexpensive torchère provides ambient light, while an articulating desk lamp offers adjustable task light at the work surface.

# Prefab Sewing Room

When fiber artist Marty Gunion decided to convert a spare bedroom into a workroom, she knew she'd need to fit at least three workstations (layout, cutting, and sewing) into the relatively small space, but she wasn't sure how best to do it.

▲ **The dark-green wall color is a soft** backdrop for the white cabinetry and the incredible array of sewing items large and small. A workable combination of task and ambient lighting distributes light at the intensities needed at each workstation.

## From Bedroom to Sewing Room

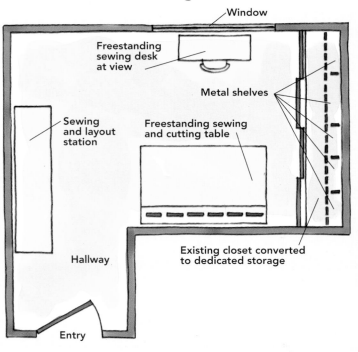

Window

Freestanding sewing desk at view

Metal shelves

Sewing and layout station

Freestanding sewing and cutting table

Existing closet converted to dedicated storage

Hallway

Entry

Enter interior designer Penny Gimbel. Recognizing that Penny needed a variety of work surfaces of varying heights and depths and lots of storage space, Penny recommended using a prefabricated closet and cabinet system, which had the twin benefits of versatility and cost-effectiveness.

The converted bedroom holds an incredible amount of storage of supplies and materials, but although the space is admittedly busy, it doesn't look cluttered. That's because some basic design principles were employed. First, there's nothing on the floor except furniture and cabinets. Second, there's a custom-designed home for every single item—from thread racks and magnetic strips for cutting tools to cabinets for long bolts and odd-shaped materials.

▲An existing closet (with mirrored sliding doors) was pressed into service for hanging fabrics and wire-drawer storage. In the foreground, an articulating task light with a magnifier in the head allows the artist to focus on fine work at the counter-high workstation.

▶Cabinet doors open to reveal deep storage at the end of the cutting station, especially useful for long bolts of fabric. The sewing station gets natural light—and the view.

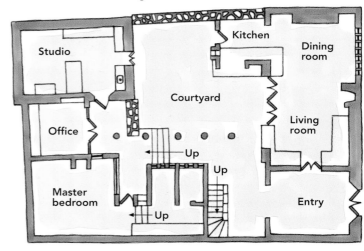

## Around the Courtyard

Studio

Kitchen

Dining room

Office

Courtyard

Living room

Master bedroom

Up

Up

Up

Up

Entry

▲▶ A small office in a renovated walled house in rural Mexico faces onto a central courtyard, as do all the other rooms on the ground floor. In a house so introspective in plan, it's only fitting that this sparse room is used primarily for reading and meditation. Materials are simple, with a pine reading desk backed by a wall-to-wall, built-in unit that holds sundry supplies behind cabinet doors. A recessed spotlight provides general illumination, while a gooseneck task lamp picks up the slack at the work surface.

# Upstairs, Downstairs

When Anne and Hayward, both political-science professors, bought a house in Santa Monica, California, one of their top priorities was to find two independent spaces where they could work at home. Working with Los Angeles architect Barbara Bestor, they chose to convert an upstairs bedroom for one study and a large closet on the lower floor (which served the master bedroom) for the other.

In the upstairs bedroom, a closet was removed and outfitted with bookcases, and an L-shaped work area was wrapped around two walls, with the long leg under the window. One of the requirements for this room was that it could also serve as a guest bedroom. This was cleverly accomplished by building in a shallow wall unit opposite the work area that conceals a Murphy bed. Next to the bed is another closet, which conceals a roll-out night table. (See the floor plan on p. 104.)

In the lower-level walk-in closet, two structural changes were made. First, space

▲In the upstairs workplace, the detailing of the shelving minimizes the vertical and support elements and accentuates the horizontal, which helps keep the eye from rising upward. This visual trick makes a low-ceilinged room appear to be higher. The upturned lip on the shelves adds to the horizontal banding, strengthens the shelves, and provides lateral stability in the event of a tremor.

◀A wraparound work surface in the upstairs workplace provides ample space for project and administrative layout and for computer work. Roll-out files are shown neatly parked below. Wide-slat wood venetian blinds control light and tie in aesthetically with the warm cherry cabinetry.

▲In the downstairs office, a new window with transoms above was installed to lighten up the converted closet. Bookshelves are staggered in the corner for more light and to allow overhead room above the printer. The designer's signature toboggan-style counter termination is visible at far right.

## Upstairs Study

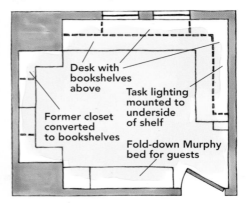

Desk with bookshelves above

Task lighting mounted to underside of shelf

Former closet converted to bookshelves

Fold-down Murphy bed for guests

was borrowed from the wall behind to create a new closet, which would also serve the connecting master bedroom. The remaining closet space could then be dedicated to workplace functions. Second, a low window was introduced into the outside wall, turning the dark, froglike closet into a princely workstation. A pocket door divides the workplace from the adjacent hall for privacy when needed, but matching built-in bookcases march through and out into the hall, effectively expanding

## Downstairs Study

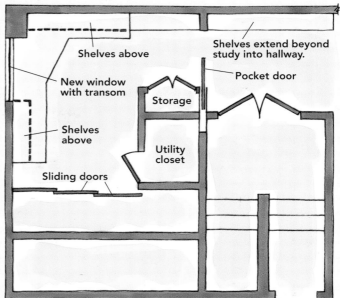

Shelves above

New window with transom

Shelves above

Sliding doors

Storage

Utility closet

Shelves extend beyond study into hallway.

Pocket door

▲ **Matching-style wood shelving marches beyond** the door of the lower office out into the hallway. The wall-supported bookshelf assembly stops short of the oak floor, giving the appearance that it's floating in space.

storage and the perceived size of the space. (See the floor plan above.)

Many design features are common to both upper and lower workplaces, including carefully proportioned, clean-lined, cherry built-in workstations; an oak strip floor; paint-grade bookshelves; and recessed lighting, which is particularly effective in rooms with low ceilings. Both rooms also feature a unique Bestor detail—turning the counter end upward "toboggan" style to screen the workstation from the view at the doorway.

A hallmark of the design is the clean, uncluttered look. This is achieved partly by linear design, but mainly by working closely with the clients to make sure there's a perfect place to store, access, and display every element in the office. In that way, it becomes a pleasure for the user to return all things to their rightful domain, which is the secret to eliminating clutter and confusion in any workplace.

▲ Custom pine wall units provide storage all around in this highly personalized study. The dark-wood antique reading table and black-shaded desk lamp offer good visual contrast against the pale wood of the cabinetry.

## Ambient Lighting

It's usually best to have a combination of focused task lighting and ambient lighting in your work space. Recessed ceiling lighting on a dimmer can provide general illumination, which can be balanced for brightness as needed. Select units with a deep-recessed lamp and a nonreflective baffle to minimize glare. If you're working in a room that doesn't have ceiling lighting, think about buying a torchiere. This is a floor lamp that's designed to light the ceiling, which, in turn, provides some ambient light in the room.

# Bigger Isn't Always Better

This remodeled home workplace was conceived as part of a complete second-floor makeover of a 1950s builder's home. Before the remodel, the upstairs was dark and constricted. By eliminating the sitting room, creating a double-height space at the entry, and adding interior windows, the entire second floor is now flooded with light. (See the floor plan below.)

By relocating a nonload-bearing partition, architect Jon Anderson was able to enlarge the master bathroom and plan a cozy little home workplace in the remaining space. Though the space is smaller than the original study, it is organized more efficiently, with a custom-built corner desk, a storage closet, and a console of cabinets built around the chimney. What hasn't changed is the great corner view out to the Sandia Mountains.

## Making the Most of a Second-Floor Remodel

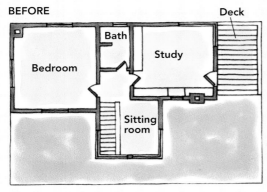

BEFORE

Deck
Bath
Study
Bedroom
Sitting room

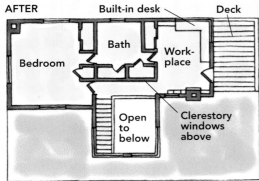

AFTER

Built-in desk
Deck
Bath
Work-place
Bedroom
Open to below
Clerestory windows above

▲ Existing corner casement windows finish out just above the counter height of the new custom workstation. Drawer fronts are made of perforated aluminum panels. Equipment that would obstruct the view is placed away from the window.

# Basement Workplaces

As discussed in chapter 1, basements are potential candidates for home workplaces because they are typically large, open spaces that are underused. The two biggest drawbacks are lack of light (and view) and possible moisture problems. If you have a walkout basement, the light problem is somewhat minimized, but in below-grade basements, you'll have to make some modifications to make the space more hospitable. A few options you might consider include opening the basement to the main level of the house (where possible), adding windows, installing a well-planned system of electrical lighting, and finishing in light colors. You'll also want to consider insulation—in walls, and especially the floor slab.

If your basement is susceptible to any water seepage, you should identify and correct the problem before considering using it for office space (or for storage space). This might entail repairing cracks in the foundation, installing foundation drains, fixing broken gutters, or applying masonry sealers. Basements can become very humid in the warmer months, which can damage supplies and sensitive computer equipment, as well as cause user discomfort. A properly

▲ Basement workplaces don't have to be dark and gloomy. This walkout basement features a project station at the large sliding window (taking advantage of the light and the view) and a separate computer workstation. Recessed ceiling luminaires provide ambient lighting.

◀Formerly a basement rec room, this uncluttered space is workplace central for a Hollywood screenwriter. The designer achieved a clean, minimalist look by hiding or screening all things unwieldy—including a printer (beneath the L-shaped desk), fax machine and office supplies (in the framed vitrine behind the workstation), and cables and wires (within the workstation).

## Concrete Floors

The concrete floors of most basements are uninsulated below the concrete. As a result, the floor typically remains cold during the winter months, even if a comfortable temperature is maintained in the basement. If you are sitting for long periods, the floor will absorb heat from your feet, and you may become uncomfortably cold. This problem can be solved by building an insulated floor above the concrete floor (as shown in the drawing on p. 173). Carpeting with a good insulating pad underneath it will also help to reduce heat loss.

◀Transom glazing and a new glass door with sidelite draw in natural light and make a connection between the inside of the basement work space and an outdoor courtyard.

sized and placed dehumidifier should solve this problem, but you'll also want to isolate the entry of moist outside air to the basement.

If you're going to renovate a basement for use as a workplace, it's a good idea to build insulated wood-frame walls around the area you'll use, including the perimeter foundation. A modest amount of heat supply will then make the space comfortable during the winter months. ■

# A Wired, Walkout Workplace

By and large, basements present a challenge for use as work space because there is typically no view and little natural light. In a walkout basement, however, there may be an opportunity for compensation. In this converted basement space, remodeler Paul Sullivan was able to introduce full-view windows by puncturing into the foundation wall, capturing light as well as a panoramic view.

Aside from the light issue, the owner (an investment banker) had one, main requirement: that the new workplace be fully equipped—a functional mirror of his Boston office—so he could work just as easily at home as at the office. (See the floor plan on the facing page.) The custom cherry cabinetry is traditional raised panel,

▲From the main command-center workstation, the fireplace, television monitor, and window are all within easy view—and all are controlled remotely. Black granite surfaces on the main workstation and around the hearth of the fireplace contrast with the cherry casework.

▲At the end of the U-shaped workstation an array of flat-panel computer monitors is tucked below a storage cabinet. The owner can use the main desk for administrative chores and paper layout, while windows to the financial world are accessed on-screen simply by a spin of the task chair.

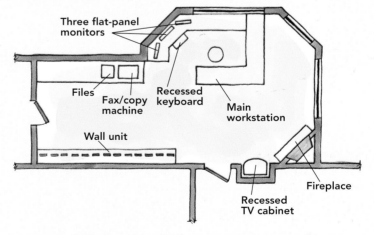

◀Recessed wall washers light the matching custom cherry wall unit, which has a bank of cabinets at ground level and ample storage for books and memorabilia in the open shelf areas above. A milled and scribed cherry wood cornice tops off the assembly.

but it is designed to accommodate hidden wiring for three flat-screen monitors behind the main workstation, a copying and fax center, a large-screen television monitor, dual-bank video players, and ethernet and other communications wiring. Extensive cabling is chased through the walls and cabinetry, where it is hidden yet accessible.

Paul went beyond office equipment in specifying electronics for remote-control, motorized window blinds and a remote-control gas-fueled fireplace. A state-of-the-art multizone sound system, which can be controlled from any location in the house, is connected to recessed speakers in the ceiling of the work space. Everything is operable and adjustable from the U-shaped command-center workstation.

**Basement Workplace**

Three flat-panel monitors

Files

Fax/copy machine

Recessed keyboard

Main workstation

Wall unit

Fireplace

Recessed TV cabinet

# Attic Workplaces

One of the great bene- fits of setting up a workplace in an attic is that it's a totally private location, remote from the hustle and bustle of the rest of the house. As with any other location, of course, there are some potential drawbacks— low headroom, limited access, temperature control, and inadequate lighting. To illustrate the challenges (and benefits) of using an attic as work space I've chosen to use the example of my own home workplace, which was developed from raw attic space in a 1930s Connecticut Cape.

I was lucky enough to have an existing oak staircase lead- ing up to the attic (see the floor plan on p. 114), and the rough plank floor was capable of withstanding the added load—an important consideration when evaluating any attic space (see the sidebar on the facing page). There were double- hung windows at each gable end, so I already had some nat- ural light. But there was no heat, insulation, lighting, or electrical power in the attic, plus I wanted to maintain about half the attic space for storage. Although the clearance at the peak (7 ft.) was a little on the low side, I didn't want to go to the expense of raising the roof—nor did I want to add dormers. The challenge was to create a highly functional,

▲ The unusual exposed cross-bracing and angular ceiling planes provide plenty of visual interest in this attic workplace in London, England. The L-shaped workstation is simple and spacious, with lots of narrow drawer storage below.

►The custom-built fluorescent-light valances behind the computer and drafting equipment provide perfect background lighting for the monitors, reducing eyestrain while also providing a well-lit back area to access the equipment ports.

◄In the author's own home workplace, workstations along the kneewalls preserve valuable headroom at the center of the attic floor.

## Beefing Up the Floor

If you're thinking of using raw attic space as your home workplace, you need to make sure that the structural members (the joists) of the existing attic floor are capable of handling live loads. Some attic floors are designed only to handle light storage and are not intended for use as living (or working) space. This problem can be remedied by adding additional structural members, but an analysis should be done by an architect or structural engineer in the planning stages. Whether or not you need to make structural modifications, plan on insulating the floor for noise control.

comfortable, and attractive space within these limitations while controlling overall costs.

Fortunately, there was enough excess power at the recently upgraded electrical panel in the basement to bring up additional lines for lighting, heating/air conditioning, and equipment use. I didn't need water upstairs, so plumbing wasn't an issue. Although I have hot-water heating in the rest of the house, I chose to heat my work space with an oil-filled, electric baseboard unit. This reduced my initial cost and allows me to control the temperature separately.

I elected to design custom furniture and lighting to make the most of the available space and to offset the low-ceiling feel. I treated the existing floor plan like a ship's galley and planned all my workstations against the low walls. Using this strategy, I was able to maintain the higher central space for standing and moving around. Because my workstations

## An Attic Workplace: Floor Plan

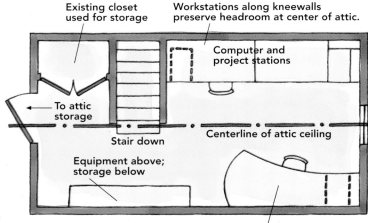

Existing closet used for storage

Workstations along kneewalls preserve headroom at center of attic.

Computer and project stations

To attic storage

Stair down

Centerline of attic ceiling

Equipment above; storage below

Meeting and administrative station

## An Attic Workplace: Section

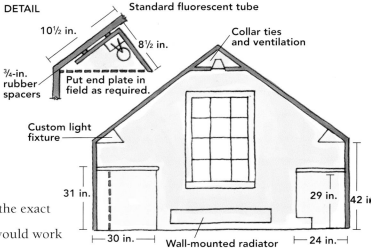

DETAIL

Standard fluorescent tube

10½ in.

8½ in.

Collar ties and ventilation

¾-in. rubber spacers

Put end plate in field as required.

Custom light fixture

31 in.

29 in.

42 in.

30 in.

Wall-mounted radiator

24 in.

▲ A rollaway keyboard tray holds a laptop computer at the administrative station, conserving valuable space in the 175-sq.-ft. attic workplace.

were going to be custom-built, I was able to plan the exact lengths, depths, and heights of the surfaces that would work best for the floor plan, and for my personal needs.

There are four workstations in my home office—computer, administrative, meeting, and project stations. My computer and project stations are actually one continuous surface with two computer stations, supported by pedestal file cabinets at the ends. My canoe-shaped combination administrative/meeting station is wide at the gathering end and narrower at the work end, conserving much-valued open floor space while adding visual interest.

I gave a lot of thought to the lighting in the remodeled attic. For ambient (general space) light, I installed overhead, recessed, incandescent fixtures at the apex, controlled by an

## Climate Control

Depending on the geographic location, attics can get very hot during the summer months. Add a full complement of heat-generating computer equipment and room temperature can quickly rise beyond the comfort level. You may be able to ventilate your work space—by opening windows or operable skylights, for example—but when you have all your equipment running, the lights are on, and it's the height of summer, you'll most likely require additional cooling. If you choose to install an air-conditioning unit, bear in mind that this will be an additional load on the power consumption within your workplace.

◀A niche within a converted attic is stylized to the max. Niches within the niche are used to their fullest extent for the odd-shaped storage items that are stock-in-trade for an interior designer. The window seat provides some relief in the tight space and also incorporates flat drawers for plans and large drawings.

▲▶ Overflow storage from a renovated attic work space in a three-floor Chicago loft is housed in glass-fronted cabinets on the adjoining landing. The door to the office is set in a partial wall, which allows the owner to close off the work space without losing the light from the windows.

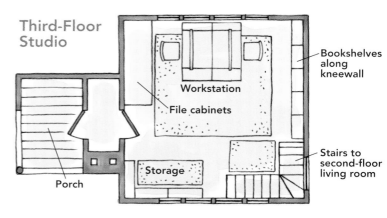

## Third-Floor Studio

Bookshelves along kneewall

Workstation

File cabinets

Stairs to second-floor living room

Storage

Porch

▲ Back-to-back tilted work surfaces on sawhorses constructed from dimensional lumber provide a drafting table and general lay-out station in a design studio atop a three-story Maine cottage. A soaring open ceiling, painted to look like a sky at sunset, accentuates the vertical, while a four-square band of windows allows views to the river below.

▲ Heat, light, power, and ventilation can make raw attic space livable, but a little more effort can make the difference between habitable space and space that's a joy to inhabit. Here, a door to an outside deck, a small square awning window at eye-level, an odd-shaped fireplace, and a bank of cabinets that ties the disparate elements together add depth, dimension, light, and views to what might otherwise have been a nondescript workplace.

electronic dimmer. For task lighting at the workstations, I integrated the lighting with the cabinetry, using custom-designed fluorescent-light valances. They're tucked neatly into the notch of the knee wall, where the pitched roof begins to rise. The light emanates below eye level and behind equipment, providing an even wash along the work surfaces, without any reflective glare. And as a big plus, the light fixtures don't take up any precious table space.

An advantage of starting with raw space is that I was able to pick all new finishes. I selected carpet, paint, and wood-work that would wear well and complement each other. I chose a rather neutral palette, with warm tones to counter-act the grayness of our long, New England winters. ■

# Light from Above

Workplaces that don't have natural light aren't pleasant places to work. If you've targeted a space that doesn't have a wall window, then perhaps you can introduce one. In cases where windows can't be inserted, such as in abutting walls, a skylight may be the answer.

Skylights with slender profiles can be inserted between rafter joists, or the joist system can be modified to accept skylight units that are wider than the standard rafter spacing within your

▲ Adding a dormer exposes the existing roof rafters as structural elements, which are then finished as part of the room. Inserting awning windows within the resulting pocket above the wall introduces natural light and ventilation.

▲ A bank of fixed skylights between the rafters floods the work area with natural light and provides a view of the treetops.

▲ A 3-ft.-sq. skylight directly over the main project station in a work space for a graphic artist introduces natural light in a room without wall windows. The light well widens as it penetrates the roof, dispersing the light through the opening and down onto the work surface.

roof. In addition to rafter spacing, you'll also have to consider roof pitch, length of span, roofing materials, and climate when you're choosing a skylight. An architect or structural engineer can help you make a proper selection.

If you're thinking of adding skylights, you'll also have to evaluate the possibility of glare and heat gain. Both can be controlled with the proper skylight system. In the case of glare, some skylights have integrated operable shading devices. Similarly, heat gain can be tempered by using operable skylights with screens. Both options are available with hand cranks, or they can be equipped with motors and remote-control devices.

# Cape Practicality

When Mike and Susan, a builder and an architect, were planning a joint work space in their new Cape-style home, efficiency, practicality, and comfort were high on their list of priorities. The location they chose was a second-floor attic space that runs the length of the house.

The access stair is close to the center of the attic space and serves as the natural divider between the workplace on one side and a guest bedroom and bath on the other (see the floor plan below). Shed-roof dormers raise the headroom on the workplace side and provide niches for the two workstations. Mike's computer/administrative station—a simple built-in counter atop a pair of filing cabinets—faces south. Susan's drafting station is on the opposite wall.

In the nondormer areas, bookshelves and vertical file cabinets are inserted into shallow niches, with a soft-seating area between. This arrangement makes good use of areas of low-headroom while preserving the central space of the attic for circulation—and maximum headroom. Cavities behind the kneewall space were outfitted with access doors to take advantage of valuable storage space that often goes unused. Double French doors at the gable end open to a railing for a connection to the great outdoors.

▲ The computer/administrative workstation is behind the bank of windows in the south-facing shed dormer.

## A Model of Efficiency

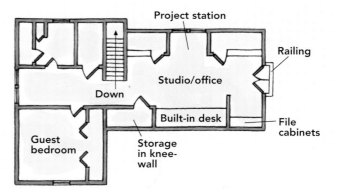

Project station

Railing

Studio/office

Down

Built-in desk

File cabinets

Guest bedroom

Storage in knee-wall

The finished floor is construction-grade pressboard (more typically used for sheathing and subflooring) treated with several coats of polyurethane. The resulting finish is economical, easy to clean, and interesting to look at. A pair of matching wrought-iron chandeliers provide ambient light under the pitched-roof ends of the workplace, adding a softening, homey touch to the environment.

▲ Shed dormers provide headroom above the workstations on either side of the attic space. Storage behind the kneewall is accessed via unobtrusive flush doors.

# Sunrooms and Porches

Sunrooms make cheery, light-filled workplaces, but it can take a good deal of work to make them habitable year-round. The first thing you need to do when converting a sunroom (or a porch) is to make sure that all surfaces exposed to the weather are properly insulated. That includes the roof, walls, and floor. Sunrooms, especially those in warmer climates, are typically constructed on concrete slabs, and you'll need to consider some type of flooring insulation for winter use. Screen rooms and porches usually have wood-framed floors elevated above ground level and are almost never insulated (see the drawing below).

## Preparing a Sunroom for a Home Workplace

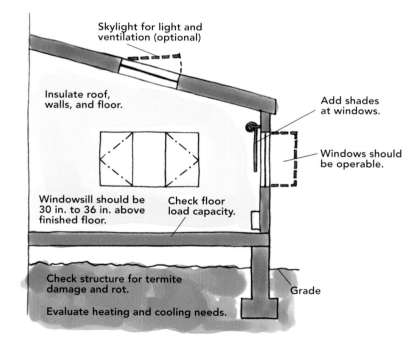

Skylight for light and ventilation (optional)

Insulate roof, walls, and floor.

Add shades at windows.

Windows should be operable.

Windowsill should be 30 in. to 36 in. above finished floor.

Check floor load capacity.

Check structure for termite damage and rot.

Grade

Evaluate heating and cooling needs.

In some parts of the country, local zoning ordinances classify porches and screened rooms in the front of a house as "verandas." These spaces are subject to less demanding setback requirements than the fully enclosed house. Be aware that if you convert this space to four-season use, it may no longer be compliant with the setback requirements. Before you begin, check with your local building official.

▲ This converted sunroom is bathed in light, with a skylight directly over the main workstation. During the summer, an overhead fan keeps the insulated space cool, while a woodburning stove compensates for heat loss through the significant areas of glass during the winter.

◄ A free-form, icy-blue glass workstation tablet provides a cool contrast to the lush landscape of the tropical rear yard, while custom, lateral file drawers tucked beneath the windowsill add more counter space without blocking the view. Shades stacked over the picture windows can be dropped as required to control penetrating sunlight.

# A Creative Workplace

When your house is on a tight urban lot, there's not much room for building an addition. So, if you want a sizable workplace, you'll have to find an existing part of the house that can be redefined for work. For Peter (a TV director and actor) and wife Roz (a volunteer for a local arts foundation), that underutilized piece of real estate was an enclosed glass porch attached to the back of the house, which was being used more as a storage shed than as living space.

The couple wanted a strong and comfortable connection between the new work space and the main living area without giving up workplace privacy. To achieve this, they replaced the existing door between the porch and the house with a full glass door and cut a hole into the rear wall of the house, into which they inserted a glass display case. The case is accessible from both sides but divided by a glass light in the center for sound control. The transparent display case brings borrowed light into

▲ Varied and creative storage solutions are a highlight of the design. Out-of-the-way deep, overhead storage bins add a major horizontal element to the space.

◀Sandblasted windows and unusual pendants are part of the overall lighting scheme—for day and night. Cabinets and built-ins on steel legs float 3 in. above the concrete floor, which decreases their visual weight.

the main space and provides a strong visual connection between the main living area and the new workplace.

The existing glass windows on the porch were replaced with sandblasted glass. The space is therefore visually screened, and daylight is evenly dispersed into the room; no shades or blinds needed here. The existing concrete floor was raised to compensate for a slight water infiltration problem. The new concrete pad was embedded with a special black paint, which was mixed in during the pour and sealed over when finished. The result is a floor that looks like slate—and one that's virtually indestructible.

One of the things Peter requested was deep storage for manuscripts. Designer Barbara Bestor satisfied this need by installing airline-style overhead storage bins, matched in materials to the overall custom cabinetry. The sharp-edged design plays nicely against the rectangular rhythms set up by the window bays and the exposed roof beams. Unusually shaped globe pendants do a nice job of lighting the room, while task lamps add illumination at the workstations.

The strong organization of active records and supplies—two key elements in most workplaces—is clearly evident in this design. Not a single pencil is left without a home, and nothing clutters the floor or surfaces. The result is a crisp, fresh workplace, always ready for creative activity.

## Enclosed-Porch Conversion

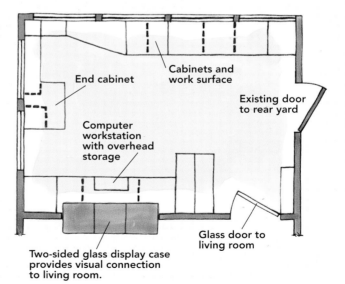

End cabinet

Cabinets and work surface

Existing door to rear yard

Computer workstation with overhead storage

Glass door to living room

Two-sided glass display case provides visual connection to living room.

# How to Control Glare

Glare can come from two sources: either directly from the light source (the sun or the bulb) or from a reflected source (usually a computer monitor). Not surprisingly, solar glare can be a real problem in sunroom workplaces. If you put a monitor in front of a window, make sure that you install good-quality, easily operable shading behind it.

If you're working at a computer, avoid surface-mounted overhead lights, which create veiling reflections. You can reduce direct glare by positioning recessed lighting behind you, though this may throw unwanted shadows onto the work surface. An alternative is to move the light below eye level (using, for example, a halogen lamp on a flexible arm). Make sure desk lamps near the monitor are well shaded (see the drawing at right).

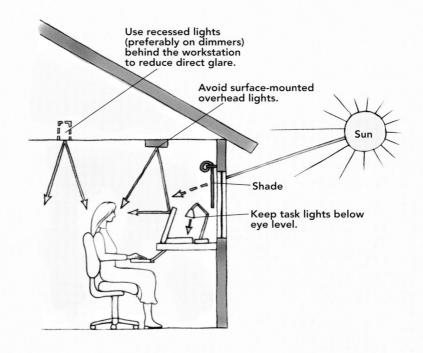

Use recessed lights (preferably on dimmers) behind the workstation to reduce direct glare.

Avoid surface-mounted overhead lights.

Sun

Shade

Keep task lights below eye level.

If you have to insulate the walls and roof, add recessed lighting and power runs when the walls are open. Evaluate heating and air-conditioning needs based on climate, exposure, and heat loads from your office equipment. You'll need to add some kind of shading device to reduce heat gain and to control glare (see the sidebar above), and you might consider adding a skylight (preferably one that is operable) for ventilation. Windows should be operable; consider thermal pane in cold climates. ▪

# High Definition: New Rooms in New Houses

If you're fortunate enough to be building a new home, you'll have an opportunity to define your workplace exactly as you want it. Without the constraints of a predetermined size or location in an existing home, you'll have far more design latitude.

Create a thorough list of your home-workplace requirements, and review it with your architect in the early planning stages. Make sure there's plenty of natural light and at least one good view. Be generous with the amount of space you allocate, keeping in mind your present needs and any plans for future expansion. Since you have the luxury of building from the ground up, you'll be able to incorporate cable runs for all kinds of communications pathways, which is a lot less expensive to do now than when the walls are closed in.

Above all, don't be afraid to give your imagination some free rein. You'll probably be spending more waking time in this room than any other in the house, so make it interesting, comfortable, and personal—just as the owners of the two workplaces on the following pages have done.

▼ **Designing a workplace** gives you the best opportunity to plan the space and run all the necessary support utilities.

## Ocean Office

The owner, an international businessman, asked Los Angeles architect Steven Kanner to design a southern California vacation home with a top-floor workplace. This would be a home-away-from-home; his main residence and office are overseas. He also wanted something that had a strong connection to the ocean and that expressed his love of all things nautical. Although his tastes could be described as modern, his wife likes more traditional styles. The resulting house is a marriage of the two—with a clearly overriding nautical theme—which explains the interesting and unusual rear elevation.

Kanner explains the rich circular-window vocabulary as a twofold metaphor: They're reminiscent of portholes and of

◀The rear elevation of the house is a marriage of styles and tastes—with an obviously nautical theme.

▲ The workplace overlooks the main living area.

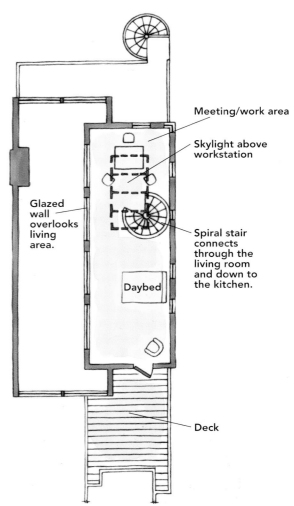

Meeting/work area

Skylight above workstation

Glazed wall overlooks living area.

Spiral stair connects through the living room and down to the kitchen.

Daybed

Deck

bubbles (both connected with water). Some windows are fixed, while others pivot around a center axis; some overlap, and some wrap around the corner of the house. All are custom-made. In privacy areas, such as bathrooms, a special coating was applied to the glass. On demand, an electric current converts the glazing from clear to translucent, eliminating the need for window shades and allowing an uninterrupted view.

The crow's-nest workplace is accessed by a turret-spiral stair, which connects through the living area and down to the kitchen (see the floor plan above). At the workplace, the stair is railed off with curved tempered glass, which adds a

◄The workstation end of the workplace features a clear, Lucite desk surrounded by classic Eames chairs. At the deck end, the couch is the perfect place to kick back.

crystalline quality to the space. The workplace is bathed in light and views—out to the sea through the portholes; down to the living area through the glazed wall; and back toward the mountains through a playfully shaped glass-and-wood-framed door, which opens to a planked viewing and sitting deck.

Clerestory glazing cuts mirror the shape of the wing-like roof cap, and a skylight penetration within the roof illuminates the work area and spiral stair. Midday sun is eliminated by a motorized panel, similar to a moon roof on a car. Point-source, low-voltage ceiling lighting takes over at night.

Kanner reports that the owner maintains the workplace just as shown in the photos, with everything shipshape all the time. The owner's personal organization has evolved to an ultimate level of minimalist precision, and the workplace therefore perfectly supports his needs—albeit in a playful southern California style. ■

▲All aboard. The curving and angular design features, draped by the ocean and horizon line behind, make it feel as though you're rolling with the waves.

▲ The exterior, showing the
entry at far left.

## The Oval Office

This home, designed by architect Barry Berkus, includes a
dedicated workplace that borrows the footprint of another,
more familiar office. Located on the ground floor and at the
end of the main entry axis, the space provides a secluded
and contemplative work environment for the owner. The
office also serves as a place to meet with clients, who
arrive at the room through a procession of grand exterior
and interior spaces.

The workplace itself has glass-paneled double doors,
which provide audible privacy but preserve a visual connection to the main house. Niches in the office provide space

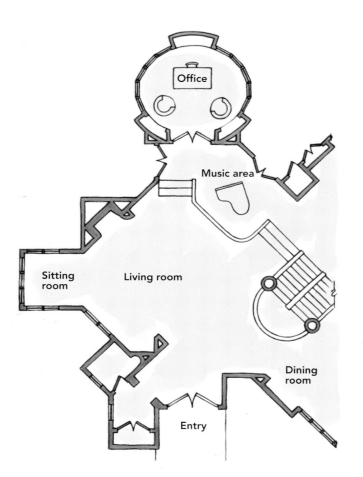

▲ Clean design lines, recessed lighting, and perimeter niches help the owner avoid clutter in this relatively small, but geometrically powerful space.

for credenza, counters, and bookshelves. By containing furniture behind the wall line, the niches also maintain the smooth, uninterrupted perimeter of the oval's deceptively small footprint. Operable casement windows to either side of the credenza niche expand the feeling of spaciousness.

Indirect lighting within a recessed ceiling coffer around the entire perimeter of the oval bounces off the smooth flat ceiling, and the room glows softly with indirect light. Recessed luminaires with wide-diffusion reflectors provide task lighting at the workstation.

A custom oval desk mirrors the overall design of the room. On the visitor side, the supporting pedestals are barrel shaped, while pencil and file drawers flank knee space on

# Finish Selection

When it comes to selecting finishes and colors for a personal space, it's difficult to provide hard-and-fast rules, but there are a few general guidelines that are appropriate for most workplaces:

• For the floor, choose a material that's durable and easy to clean and that a task chair can roll on without difficulty. If you install carpet, ask for a material that is "low-static." Deep-pile carpet is not a good idea in a work environment.

• On the walls, avoid anything that's delicate or hard to clean. Vinyl wall coverings are easy to maintain, but choose a color and texture with a residential character. Avoid wild patterns, which can be distracting.

• Avoid colors that are too bright or too dark. Hot and vibrant colors tend to be wearing on the eyes, while dark colors may reduce ambient light. A 20 percent light-absorbent pastel finish is easy on the eyes and is more forgiving for scuffs and marks.

• Colors, textures, and finishes picked independently don't always

▲ In a work environment, the general rule is that you want neutral, light, and unobtrusive colors. In this room with multiple workstations, custom cabinetry and matching colors ensure a uniform appearance.

work well as a group. Before you commit to your interior decor, gather samples of everything, including furniture finishes, and look at them together. If you need to, you can always seek professional assistance.

the work side. Objects from the owner's collection of primitive art are prominently displayed within the credenza niche, adding the finishing touch to this highly personalized home workplace. ■

# Adding On

# 5

▶An artist's studio attached to the rear of a garage in historic Concord, Massachusetts, overlooks a patio and the main house beyond.

If your building lot (and your budget) can accommodate it, you might want to consider creating a workplace by adding onto your existing home. Taking this route is usually more expensive than reconfiguring existing space because you're typically building from the ground up—you'll need everything from the foundation to the roof. Money aside, there are several benefits to this approach, including greater privacy and protection for your workplace, greater freedom of design, and the ability to create a separate entrance.

Before embarking on a workplace addition, you'll need to get approval from your local building department. Most towns have regulations about how close you can build to property lines (see the sidebar

◀A grand, three-story addition on the Connecticut shore has it all: a meeting room on the ground floor, a private home workplace on the second floor, and a third-floor library and observatory.

# Understanding Setbacks

To maintain safe access to exits in case of fire, separation between neighbors, and appearance, almost all residential communities have adopted regulations requiring mandatory minimum distances between the building line and the property line—otherwise known as setbacks.

Setback distances may be different for front, side, and rear yards. They also may vary from community to community and even from one residential zone to another. The best way to ascertain setback requirements on your lot is to visit the local building department, with either a lot plan or the legal designation number of your lot. Once you know where the setbacks are located,

▲The rear yard of this remodeled 1940s bungalow had just enough room for a small studio addition nestled into a south-facing courtyard.

you can determine whether a certain-size addition will fit or whether it must be reshaped or downsized.

above). They may also be concerned about the appearance of the finished addition, especially if you live in a historic district. Depending on the size of the lot and the size of the existing home, there may be limitations on the size of the addition. Most important, how you intend to use your workplace will be of particular interest to local building authorities.

Once you get approval for the addition, you'll have to live through the construction process—

▲ A second-floor addition above a remodeled garage gives the owner, an archeologist, total privacy from the main house.

and the weeks or even months of disruption that goes along with it. Landscaping gets disturbed, pathways around the house turn to mud, and utilities may occasionally be cut off. The existing structure is also affected, even if it is only to tap utilities or connect a passageway from new to old. And, of course, additional costs are not unusual.

When all's said and done, the pain of the process gives way to the pleasure of use as well as the pride of accomplishment. In this chapter, we'll look at the two most common types of workplace additions: those at the rear or side of the house and those that are connected to the garage. ■

# Rear and Side Additions

A rear or side addition is commonly a one-level affair, typically with a separate exterior entrance and a direct connection between the new wing and the main residence. More often than not, the connection is through the kitchen, though sometimes the new entry serves as a forked connection, leading to either the new home workplace or the main living area of the house.

Whether you choose the rear or side of the house will depend on the particular configuration of your lot and

▼This wing addition to a 19th-century farmhouse is connected to the house by a covered walkway. Clerestory windows atop the workplace provide overhead ambient light, while operable double-hung windows at the work surface offer a view over the courtyard. Translucent pleated shades can be lowered as required to reduce glare.

home. For example, if you have a wide lot, with a small rear yard, a side addition makes more sense. Rear additions tend to be more common because there's usually more available space behind the house than there is on the side. Also, since a rear-yard addition is typically not visible from the road, zoning-enforcement officials are less likely to find reasons why a specific plan doesn't conform to regulations.

## From Lean-To to Studio

Most workplace additions are built from scratch, but some involve the conversion of an existing structure. Such was the case with the artist's studio addition in Patterson, New York, shown on pp. 138-139. When the house was built 25 years earlier, the owners planned for a future rear porch and had the contractor continue the roofline beyond the rear wall of the house (see the drawing at left). This area was never completed, but with the roof in place and otherwise open, it became the logical choice to create a modest, new studio for wife Nancy, who is a fine-arts teacher and professional artist.

Because the house was built into the side of a hill, the floor level of the studio had to be excavated. The existing rear entry to the house was reworked into a connecting vestibule, with steps down into the new space. After excavation, a slab was poured and a perimeter block retaining wall constructed; adding a stud wall atop the retaining wall enclosed the space. Nancy's husband, Bill, an architect, took

### A Lean-To Addition

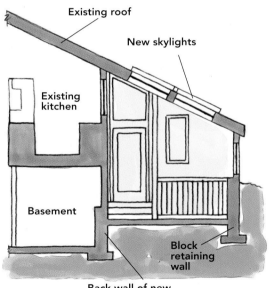

Existing roof

New skylights

Existing kitchen

Basement

Block retaining wall

Back wall of new studio/existing wall of house

▲Natural light pours in from every direction in this artist's studio. The perimeter foundation ends halfway up the wall, providing shelf space all around the room.

advantage of the different thicknesses of block and stud wall to create a wood-dressed shelf all the way around the interior of the new studio at wainscot height.

What was the exterior rear wall of the house was refinished with drywall to become a spacious display wall. To preserve light and views at the kitchen window, which now overlooks the new space, and to bring in more natural light, Nancy and Bill introduced two 4-ft. by 4-ft. skylights into the roof—one fixed and the other operable. The operable unit provides fresh air for the studio and flow-through ven-

◄The kitchen window overlooks the interior of the studio but also has eye-level views through the added skylights. The high wall below is the artist's main display area.

▲Flooring is vinyl composition tile, a relatively inexpensive, durable, and easy-to-maintain material. Steps lead up to the first floor of the house.

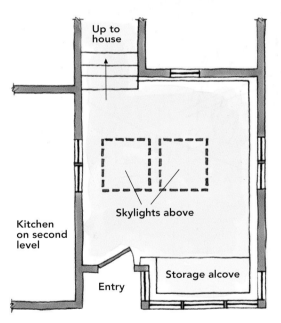

**Up to house**

**Skylights above**

**Kitchen on second level**

**Entry**

**Storage alcove**

tilation for the kitchen when its windows are open. A full-lite entry door and operable transom above add additional light and ventilation.

To the left of the door, the owners outfitted an alcove with stock kitchen cabinetry and a plastic laminate counter. In the peak area above the niche, a built-in cabinet provides deep storage. Recessed and pendant lighting illuminate the space at night, but during the day natural light is more than adequate. All in all, the new studio is quite a step up for Nancy, whose previous studio was a former chicken coop in a barn on the property. ■

## To the Lighthouse

Here's another example of a workplace addition built upon an existing structure—but this time on a much grander scale. The owner of a residence on the Connecticut shore asked friend and architect David Austin to pay him a visit to help plan "a few small changes."

In the process of walking through the house and around the property, the owner brought the architect into an adjacent one-floor structure

▲Seen from the backyard, the three-story addition is to the left of the house. (For a close-up view, see p. 132.)

◄The wood ceiling brackets and brass light fixtures in the first-floor meeting room call to mind the detailing of a sailing ship from a bygone era.

▲The second-floor workplace is built-in under a window that faces the water. This level connects to the second floor of the main house.

bursting at the seams with books. "I don't know what I'm ever going to do with them all," joked the owner. Back at the office, David came up with the idea—at the time, really just a playful proposal—to convert the one-room side building into a three story workplace and library tower, reminis-

▲The library is on the top floor with a view in all directions. A glass block floor allows light to penetrate deep into the well of the tower.

**Lighthouse Workplace**

Down to first-floor meeting room

Up to third-floor library and observatory

Open to below

Second floor

To main house

Computer workstation

Built-in book-shelves above; drawers below

cent of a lighthouse. Upon presenting the idea to the owner, it was matter-of-factly accepted as part of the "minor changes."

The first floor of the addition, conveniently accessed from the street, serves as a meeting room for business associates (and alternately as a family den). The second floor, which connects to the bedrooms, is a fully appointed workplace; although the owner has offices in town, he finds himself doing more work at home lately. The top floor is a combination library and lookout observatory, with a panoramic view of Long Island Sound.

The most notable aspect of the design is the light well that penetrates down to the ground floor. The topmost level has a glass-block floor so that none of the light from above

▲ The alternating-step stair connects all three levels, serving as a space-saving design feature. It takes a little getting used to, but unlike on a ladder, you can descend safely facing forward.

is blocked as it filters down to the old ground-floor book room. To connect all three levels internally, the architect borrowed the idea of an alternate stepladder system used in warehouses. The advantage of this design is that the ladder fits within a tight footprint in the well in significantly less space than would be required for a standard stairway.

The design reflects the owner's passion for nautical themes, with specific detailing reminiscent of boats, including a polished brass stair railing that connects all three levels, varnished mahogany on the inside of all openings with lac-quered white frames, and brass flush door pulls and rings. The effect is as though you are below deck on an early 20th-century yacht.

No matter how modest or how magnificent, the thread that connects all highly functioning workplaces is the level of organization. In this three-story workplace, every single element has a home planned for it and there's no unnecessary clutter, which is the secret to keeping any workplace shipshape and productive. ■

# Four Corners

Workplace wings of new houses lay out similar to additions—they're connected to the house but have a separate entrance. This workplace tower on the corner of a new house in rural northern California feels so much like an addition that I've opted to group it with other added spaces.

After living in Los Angeles for more than 20 years, a new telecommuting job gave Joel and his wife, Janice, an opportunity to fulfill their dream of country living. So they bought a piece of land in rural Sonoma County and set upon the journey of building a new custom-designed home.

From a stylistic point of view, the couple were charmed by the elegant simplicity of the board-and-batten farmhouses dotting the surrounding countryside. The resulting design by architect Patti Motzkin is a mixture of local farm architecture and elements of the Craftsman style. The plan is simple—public space in a large central core with two bedrooms and a bath

▲ The corner workplace tower form is derived from local agricultural water towers. A door leads directly onto the patio, which is screened by shrubbery and provides a private outdoor workplace for the owner.

located in three of the corners; the fourth corner is Joel's home workplace.

The idea for raising the roof of the workplace wing came again from the style of local agricultural water towers. The vaulted interior not only provides more apparent volume but also acts as a wind chimney.

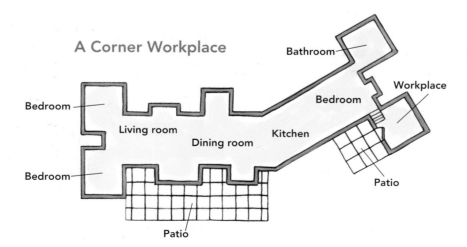

## A Corner Workplace

Bathroom

Workplace

Bedroom

Bedroom

Bedroom

Living room

Dining room

Kitchen

Patio

Patio

◀The airy interior, enhanced by the choice of light wood cabinetry, offers a great view of the rolling countryside. The flooring is concrete, laid out on a 4-ft. grid.

▼The counter height for the main computer workstation can be adjusted depending upon the needs of a particular project and the owner's personal comfort.

Manually operated windows at the top of the tower can be opened to take advantage of the nearby sea breezes, pulling hot air up and out of the tower. A large ceiling fan helps push the air along.

Following the natural contours of the land, the floor of the workplace tower is a few steps down from the main living space. A door leads directly to a private patio, which becomes an outdoor extension of the workplace, weather permitting.

Custom cabinetry finishes off the interior of the room with abundant shelving, cabinetry, and work surfaces. The main computer workstation is height adjustable, providing continuous counter space when in the low position.

▲ From the street, you'd never know that there's a highly original workplace addition behind the sunroom.

## Writing Studio in the Round

Whether you're adding a work space, a bedroom, or any other room, one of the main challenges is to make the addition fit in with the existing house and with the neighborhood. Viewed from the front, the house featured here (owned by a cultural anthropologist) appears to be like any another traditional American home, complete with basketball hoop over the porch. But go around the back and it's a different story.

Although the owner wished to maintain the traditional appearance of the facade, he wanted his new home workplace to speak more to his life and career. He also wanted privacy, a place to display some of the artifacts he'd collected over the years, and a well-equipped personalized work area, which would afford him quick access to the sizable book collection he uses for research.

Architect Travis Price came up with a unique scheme: to convert the existing greenhouse sunroom at the side of the house into a relaxed reading room and meeting area, which

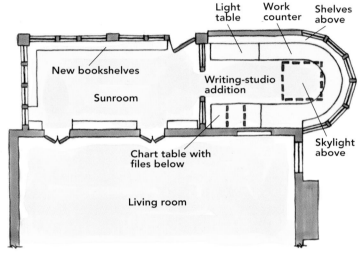

◄In back, the skylit cylinder addition dominates the right-hand end of the house. A narrow band of windows allows a peek at the wonders stored inside.

## Sunroom and Writing Studio

Light table
Work counter
Shelves above

New bookshelves

Sunroom

Writing-studio addition

Chart table with files below

Skylight above

Living room

would simultaneously serve as the transition space between the home and a new, cylindrical writing studio addition. Price borrowed the unusual form of the addition from that of a sacred Navajo *kiva*, or domed space beneath the ground, which to the Navajo represents the womb or belly button of the earth.

Within the dome and directly above the new work area, the owner's vast library is stored on inward stepping shelves that encircle the walls. At the pantheon-like pinnacle, a pyramidal cap allows natural light to pour down into the dome and onto the work surfaces. Books are accessed by a telescoping ladder.

▲ The converted sunroom provides soft seating and storage, and serves as the processional transition to the main event—the *kiva*-like work hub.

The rear yard looks out upon other houses in an urban setting, and since the intention of the design was to turn mind's eye inward, the architect introduced a window sliver at eye height, partially around the perimeter of the drum. On the exterior, maturing vines will eventually cover the sliver, allowing the owner to "see out without really seeing anywhere," as Price puts it.

The desk surface is supported on brackets to allow leg and rolling room all around. The surface itself is pulled away from the wall, so that wiring and cables can be easily dropped through anywhere along the back edge. The end surfaces of the U-shaped workstation are slightly higher for map reading and for use of a standing-height light table. Above the workplace and around the drum, the owner displays the ancient artifacts that he has collected from remote locations all over the world. ■

▲Inside the *kiva*, the upper walls are ringed with books while down at workstation level the owner displays the tapestries and other artifacts that he has collected from all over the world. The custom cherry and maple-striped floor—a tapestry in wood—is an interesting counterpoint to the tapestries on the wall.

# A Weaver's Workplace

When Patti and her husband, Fred, bought their house in Berwick, Maine, it had two main attractions—it was affordable, and there was enough space for the two of them to run their separate home-based businesses. Patti is a professional artist and weaver, while Fred has his own woodworking business, which he runs from an outbuilding on the property. Patti

▲ Double privacy doors, with inset panels handcrafted by husband Fred, lead from the house to the addition. When the doors are open, the new wing becomes an extension of the ground floor of the house, and the double width allows Patti to move large art works and equipment through with ease.

initially worked out of a large room in the house, but as business prospered she began to think seriously about building her own studio.

Rather than construct another freestanding building, architect Ann Whitney recommended that Patti build out from the end of the main house, thereby preserving open space in the rear yard. Ann came up with a plan for a new, attached, 20-ft. by

◄Standing shelves at the far end of the studio hold cones and spools of yarn within easy reach of the two looms.

▲At the opposite end of the workplace, the administrative/project station tucks under the low ceiling below the loft space.

30-ft. studio space with a partial loft above that added more living space.

Patti had three priorities for the design of the addition: an abundance of natural light; a plan for keeping her feet warm (she works in stocking feet because shoes get in the way of loom work); and a durable, easy-to-clean floor (she moves the loom around a lot).

A bank of large, south-facing windows satisfied the first priority, illuminating

Patti's work and heating up the work space. To keep Patti's feet warm, radiant hot-water heat was installed in the slab floor. Ann solved the floor-maintenance problem by specifying a chemical stain treatment for the slab. The chemicals in the stain reacted with the lime in the concrete, resulting in a pleasant patina, and the slab was then sealed to create a scratch-resistant, durable, and attractive surface that's easy to keep clean.

## Woodworker's Heaven

When your at-home business is woodworking, it's clear that this isn't the kind of work that will fit in a closet or a shared bedroom. You need space. And if you need a design studio and computer workstation as well as a workshop, you need a lot of space, preferably in separate parts of the building (see the floor plans on the facing page).

Joe Mirenna is a teacher by day with a side business as a furniture maker. When he built an addition onto his existing home in Madison, Wisconsin, Joe arrived at a two-level solution for his workplace requirements. The woodworking area sits slightly above grade, on a pier-and-beam floor; an attic area above provides space for a design studio and small crafts work space. The two spaces are connected by an interesting spiral stairwell, which sports a windowed view down into the workshop. Joe was fortunate enough to have a wide building lot, with ample room for construction of the addi-

▲ The main floor woodworking area makes good use of the open shed-roof ceiling for easy movement of overhead equipment and wood-work materials. The window to the attic office is visible at top center.

▲ The neatly planned attic is home to various workstations—including computer, administrative, and project—in a U-shaped configuration.

◄The two levels are connected by the spiral stair, which was built by the owner. At the top of the stair, a seating area tucked in under the skylight provides just enough room for a rustic rocking chair.

## Two-Level Workshop

**WORKSHOP**

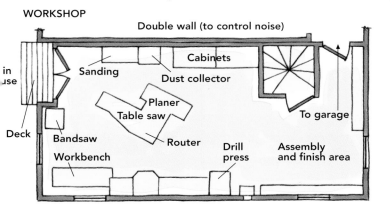

Double wall (to control noise)

Cabinets

Sanding

Dust collector

in use

Deck

Planer

Table saw

Bandsaw

Router

Workbench

Drill press

Assembly and finish area

To garage

**UPSTAIRS OFFICE**

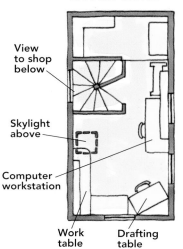

View to shop below

Skylight above

Computer workstation

Work table

Drafting table

tion, without impinging upon side-yard setback requirements.

At the main level, Joe designed the 16-ft. by 20-ft. room with a high, open-pitched ceiling. This allows him to openly distribute—and easily relocate—ductwork for the dust collection system. It also makes it a lot easier to maneuver full-dimension lumber and sheets of plywood around the work space. The upper-level attic contains traditional computer equipment for CAD drawing and printing, a multipurpose work surface, and a one-person sitting area for banjo-playing and relaxation.

The spiral stair connector is located in a 5-ft.-by-5-ft. vertical column. The entire wood assembly was constructed by Joe, whose love of wood is evident in the finishes of his crow's-nest attic work space. The operable skylight and double-hung windows provide abundant natural light, views, and flow-through ventilation from prevailing summer breezes. ■

◀Floor-to-ceiling glass on the southern elevation offers dramatic views from the ridge location of what has come to be known as the "moon-walker" house.

## An Office on Stilts

Take an innovative architect, a breathtaking location, and a homeowner who wants an office with a view and you've got the recipe for a one-of-a-kind home workplace. David is a veterinarian who does administrative work at home. He asked architect Travis Price to design an addition that would take advantage of the ridge location of the existing home, which offers a dramatic, panoramic overlook. On a clear night David especially enjoys watching the moon move across the star-lit sky. Thus instructed, the architect set out to design a building that not only makes the most of the view but is also a lyrical metaphor of the celestial orb itself.

In the plan, the addition is a sliver projection off the main house, set on stilts to compensate for the steep drop-off of the terrain immediately below. The first level houses a master bathroom addition; David's office is on the top level. A narrow hallway connector, glazed both sides, separates the

### Office Addition

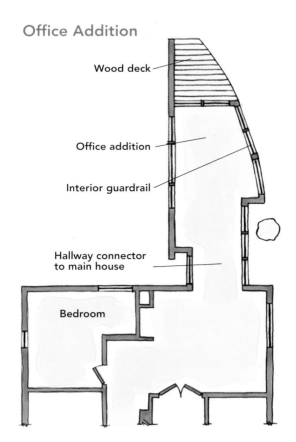

Wood deck

Office addition

Interior guardrail

Hallway connector to main house

Bedroom

◄The north elevation buffers the wind
and stands as a sculptural tableau.

addition from the home—which is a key design feature, acting as the mental demarcation between home and workplace. The south elevation captures the panoramic view with floor-to-ceiling sliding doors that form a virtual glass wall. The north elevation buffers the home from prevailing winds by use of a concrete wall, punctured only by horizontal window strips at key locations. This arrangement provides for excellent passive solar gain. The wall edge terminates in a

▲Inside the top-floor workplace, wraparound glazing on the narrow footprint, a cloud-covered ceiling, and a spectacular view contribute to the walking-on-air effect.

►Glass shelving supported by thin cables makes the objects placed upon them appear to float.

graceful curve, symbolic of a moonlike wax or wane.

In the work area, Price made good use of tensile cable—vertically, to hold glass shelves, and horizontally, to act as safety rails across the sliding doors. An upper handrail, which needed to be more substantial, is steel, chromed and custom curved into a wavelike roll. Tempered glass used for the desk surface is virtually invisible, allowing an uninterrupted view through to the outside. The ceiling is painted to resemble faint wisps of cloud cover. At the end of the sliver, sliders lead out onto an open deck, for the complete open-air effect. All elements taken together, "You feel as though you are walking on a cloud," says Price. Look at the photos and be your own judge. ■

▲The curved front edge of the tempered-glass work surface, echoed by the guardrail behind, continues the transparent, free-flowing motif of the design.

# Garage Additions

▲ An attic workplace over a two-car garage is used for general administrative work and as meeting space. The main entry (under the cross-gable) leads to the main house to the left or upstairs to the workplace. In this way, business visitors don't have to go through personal living space to get to the workplace.

Home workplace additions are sometimes combined with a new or expanded garage. The underlying logic is that the garage (new or existing) is already a separate wing of the house and any addition or reconfiguration will have less impact on the main house. Also, since the approach to the garage is vehicular, visitors by car will arrive right at the entry to the home workplace. This separate entry is usually easy to develop along with the overall plan; in some cases, a grand shared entry can be created, which leads either to the upper-level addition, or into the main living area. This can be separate from the main entry, or it can become the main entry, depending upon the overall plan.

▶ Inside, a central entry stair separates the space above the garage into a sitting area (on the left) and a workstation niche (at right).

The options for the garage home workplace vary from simply building on top of a garage to razing the existing garage and building an entirely new structure. In some cases, the garage is enlarged, perhaps from a one-car to a three-car garage, and then the home workplace is planned within it or developed on top of the enlarged footprint. Arts- or crafts-based home workplaces tend to remain on the first floor, perhaps because it's easier to move supplies in and out at ground level, whereas word-based workplaces often migrate upstairs.

If the workplace is in a detached garage, the approvals process usually becomes more involved. As a rule, the larger the land parcel and the more rural the setting, the more relaxed the permit process will be. No matter what, check your planning ideas with local governing authorities before you plant the first shovel into the ground. ■

# Heating and Cooling

Because climate, solar orientation, and construction vary so widely, temperature control of a home workplace addition has to be analyzed on a case-by-case basis. Once you've decided where your workplace will be located and what's going to be in it, an analysis of heating and cooling requirements should be performed—either by a professional engineer or by a heating and cooling contractor. Then, depending on your particular circumstances, you'll know whether you should extend your existing heating and cooling system or whether you will require standalone units for the new space.

In either case, you should consider separate controls within the new workplace—for comfort, operating savings, and energy conservation. You may want to put the workplace area on a setback thermostat. Also consider the effect of introducing any new system on space and view. For instance, the addition of a baseboard radiator may reduce floor space, or a window air conditioner may obscure the only view of the outside. In the latter case, a low-profile unit or mounting the unit through the wall can preserve your view.

◀In this small, well-insulated one-room addition, the owner was able to tap into the existing forced-air heating and air-conditioning system of the house, saving money that could be applied to lighting systems and finishes.

▲ The new two-story workplace studio (at right) was designed to complement the existing house and to conform to the town's setback requirements. The studio is a conversion of a weathered-shingle, one-story garage.

## Can I Move the Walls?

The decision to open, move, or modify an existing wall in a house should be made with caution—and with some knowledge of structural engineering. Some walls, both exterior and interior, are load bearing: they are holding up part of the structure above. These walls can be opened or removed, but not without special construction techniques and the introduction of other structural members that will do the work in place of the wall. The same applies if you are planning to add a window or door to a load-bearing exterior wall.

If you plan to move or cut openings in walls, you may affect the overall building structure. Unless you are knowledgeable about construction, you should consult a licensed architect or structural engineer before proceeding.

## Getting Approved

When Dick, a sculptor and furniture maker, and his wife decided to relocate from New York to the historic seaside arts community of Rockport, Massachusetts, an existing one-story, two-car garage on their new property seemed like an excellent candidate for conversion to a studio workplace. But when Dick asked architect Ben Nutter to make a preliminary foray to the town to discuss the proposed conversion, the project hit a snag.

## Converted and Connected

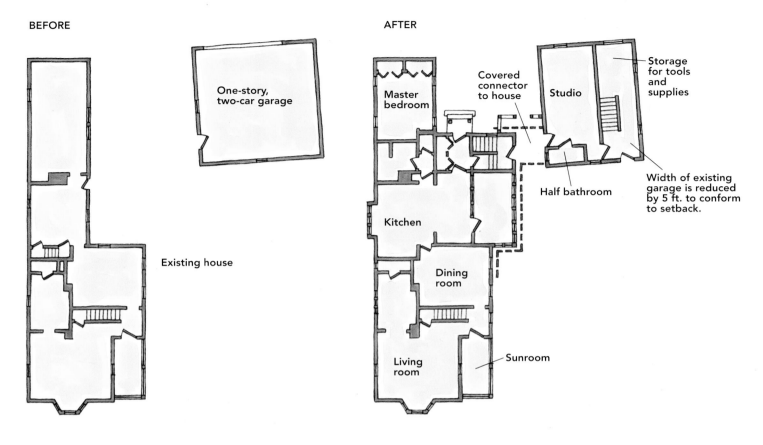

**BEFORE**

One-story, two-car garage

Existing house

**AFTER**

Master bedroom

Covered connector to house

Studio

Storage for tools and supplies

Kitchen

Half bathroom

Width of existing garage is reduced by 5 ft. to conform to setback.

Dining room

Living room

Sunroom

It turned out that the existing garage didn't conform to the town's current zoning laws—namely, part of the building sat within a now-mandated 10-ft. setback that had been established after the garage was built. There was no objection to leaving the garage as is, of course, but permission to change and expand its use was another matter.

After some discussion a compromise was reached. The owner agreed to make the footprint of the garage smaller, trimming it back by 5 ft. on the setback side to comply with zoning. In turn, the town allowed the owner to make changes to the use, recapture lost ground-floor space on an added second floor, and connect the adapted structure to the existing house (see the floor plans above).

◀Tools and supplies surround the sculptor, shown here applying the finishing touches to one of his projects.

▲The back view of the garage. The overhead hoist is used to lift supplies and furniture to the second floor (which doubles as a guest bedroom for when children and grandchildren come to visit).

The new studio was carefully designed by Nutter to complement the existing 1883 Gothic Revival house. Windows, doors, trim, and siding were all detailed to be compatible with the main building. Inside, the modest studio houses Dick's work area, with benches, table saw, and everyday tools and supplies. An adjacent first-floor bay contains additional tool and materials storage.

Dick has had hip- and knee-replacement surgery, so his mobility was an important consideration in the design of the workplace. The stairway to the second floor is extra wide with shallow riser height, and the studio also includes a half-bath. The covered connector ensures a smooth and comfortable transition from home to workplace regardless of the weather. ■

# Making the Connection

As part of an overall remodeling of their Colonial-style home, located on a hilltop site in North Andover, Massachusetts, the owners asked architect Luis Lobao of Luna Design Group to expand their existing garage to hold three cars. The previously unfinished and now expanded attic space would then be completed for use as a spacious home workplace. One of the keys to the design was to provide an easy internal connection between the house and the workplace. But the owners also wanted a way to usher visitors directly into the office from the parking area at the front entry of the house.

Architect Lobao solved the entry problem by introducing a grand stair tower as a connector between the existing house and

▲The top of the stair tower opens to a gracious landing foyer, which leads into a denlike reception area beyond. The owner's workstation is screened from view at the far end of the attic space.

◄The computer station is tucked into the corner, which makes good use of the deep space and preserves the panoramic view of treetops, water, and valley. Storage space is expanded into the kneewall cavity and trimmed in matching Colonial-style molding.

◄The hallway commute from work back to home is brief, scenic, and there's never any traffic.

## Office Above the Garage

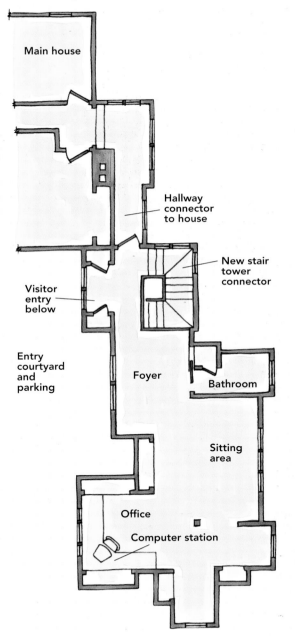

Main house

Hallway connector to house

New stair tower connector

Visitor entry below

Entry courtyard and parking

Foyer

Bathroom

Sitting area

Office

Computer station

the new, expanded garage. Business visitors have direct access to the office from the driveway parking area, through separate double-entry doors into the stair tower. The owners have interior access to the workplace through a hallway connector on the second floor (see the floor plan at right).

Inside the attic space, Lobao created a spacious entry foyer and a comfortable seating area where the owners can conduct their business meetings in a casual, homey atmosphere. Task lamps, sconces, and recessed ceiling-mounted lights provide balanced illumination throughout the workplace. The office work area itself continues the relaxed design, with pastel-green walls that soothe the eye and an Oriental rug that softens the hardwood floor and absorbs sound. And if work gets too much, there's always that great view.

◀▼The back of the house (below), which was not subject to such rigorous historic review, contrasts dramatically with the more formal and classic front (left). Pastel-colored stucco panels on the main house are repeated on the studio addition, which is connected to the house by a pergola-covered walkway.

## A Historic Addition

A workplace addition in a historic district has to conform to some strict regulations, which typically dictate not only the size of the addition but also its color and style. When Hans, an artist/illustrator and owner of the house featured here, was evaluating the property for a suitable studio location, he hired Boston architect Gary Wolf to help him come up with a renovation plan that would work for him as well as for the town. The house is in the Northbridge district of Concord, Massachusetts (where the "shot heard round the world" was fired in 1775).

◀▲The main workstation in the studio, a simple flat surface supported by wooden sawhorses, looks out upon additions to the back of the house and to the peaceful yard and sunken patio.

Wolf targeted an existing garage at the side of the house for the new studio. There was a room at the back of the garage, at one time used as a study, but it was neither big enough nor bright enough for the owner's needs. Wolf proposed that the side building be razed, and in its place a new garage and wider studio be built, replicating the style of the original house and connected to it via a pergola-covered open walkway. A small addition was also planned for the back of the house, which was not subject to

# A Studio Addition

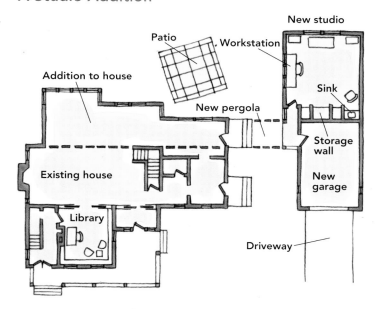

▲The owner wanted a clear separation between the place where he does his illustration work and the place where he pays bills and attends to other administrative tasks. Space was found in the library off the entry hall in the main house.

the same strict regulations as the front. Modifications on the back side could be a bit more playful, including a geometrical panel design in pastel colors, which was continued onto the side of the studio (see the floor plan above).

The architect chose a simple form for the new studio, with a high ceiling dormered over the main workstation to bring in more natural light. The picture window faces north, overlooking the back of the house and a sunken patio. The wall adjoining the garage is floor-to-ceiling deep storage to accommodate flat art of various sizes and miscellaneous supplies. Hans requested a sink in the corner so he wouldn't

## Storage for Special Project Documents

Drawings, maps, photographic archives, and other specialized documents can be difficult to store because they come in such a variety of sizes and don't always fit standard files and cabinetry. You have two options: Custom-build shelves or cabinets to fit, or buy storage units that are made for large-format or nonstandard documents. These are often sold through stores that specialize in providing products to a particular industry.

▲▲A wall of deep storage accommodates flat files of the artist's work.

have to traipse into the house to wash his brushes. In its simplicity and openness, the space is flexible enough to allow for any future changes in arrangement the artist might care to make. ▪

# 6

# A Place of Your Own

▶This simple studio was designed for an artist who didn't want to feel out of touch with the outside surroundings.

For many people who work at home, an outbuilding on the premises is the ultimate home workplace. Maybe it's the "Walden Pond" appeal, which conjures up self-reliance, the grace of solitude, and perhaps even a deeply embedded back-to-nature calling. Working at home, even in a shared space, is an act of independence. Working in a dedicated space, a place that's just for you, is another step up the ladder of independence. But working in a little building, disconnected from the world, is the closest thing we mortals may ever have to a spiritual float on earth. Those who have the luxury of seriously considering an outbuilding for their new home workplace are blessed. Ask any one of them who has managed to make the pilgrimage to their little piece of heaven on earth. ■

◀A balance of tall, narrow windows and a band of tiny clerestories admits plenty of natural light yet doesn't take up valuable wall space, which is used for temporary displays in this high-ceilinged artist's studio.

# Converting an Existing Outbuilding

If you want to create a workplace that's separate from the house, you have two options: build from scratch or convert an existing outbuilding. Compared with new construction, an outbuilding conversion or renovation is usually fraught with less difficulty because the enclosural shell is already there in full or in part. The building may additionally have power running to it, and perhaps an adjacent driveway or parking area. That said, most outbuildings will require significant effort to make them habitable and functional for home workplace use.

To begin with, the structure should be examined as carefully as if you were planning to buy it. Structural integrity, water and drainage, and the presence of hazardous materials all have to be considered. An older shed or outbuilding will most likely need some reconstructive work, in addition to surface improvements. Size is obviously important as well in evaluating the suitability of an outbuilding, which gets back to the first basic principle of workplace planning introduced in chapter 1—namely, *know your needs*.

▲ A spacious, well-lit country loft filled with personal charm, with a direct connection to an outside deck and the main house beyond, makes a warm and comfortable home workplace.

◄ The upstairs of this converted barn is roomy enough for workstations for two, with a conference table in between and storage set along the low perimeter wall to conserve headroom in the center of the space. The windows at the far end of the room open onto the stairway.

◀▲Garages are good candidates for conversion to home workplaces. A drop ceiling of plywood panels and battens can be installed to conceal joists, wires, and pipes, as in the writer's studio above. Alternatively, the structural framework, trusses, and the underside of the roof deck can be left exposed to add charm and height to the space, as shown in the architect's office at left.

Finally, you'll have to pay the building department a visit before you get too far along with your plans. The old canning shed on the property might not pass muster for a home-workplace permit—depending again upon what goes on in and around the premises; if it doesn't conform to cur-

◄This compact outbuilding workplace is a study in storage. Storage walls serve as dividers between the entry and meeting areas, while a ladder leads to a catwalk in the open-vaulted ceiling area, providing access to yet more storage.

rent setback requirements for living space, you may not be granted a permit as-of-right. If the outbuilding is within a designated historic town or is listed on a landmark registry, it could take considerably more time and money to make the conversion than you may have initially expected. It's best to know all possible obstacles in advance.

## A Garage Office

Freestanding garages make good candidates for conversion to home workplaces because they are often underutilized

## Get Permission First

Although you may think you have enough land to construct the workplace you want, it might not be feasible because of utility obstructions, zoning regulations, or other requirements. Before you get too far along with your plans, pay a visit to the local building department. Let them know what you are thinking about constructing; they may raise issues you haven't considered.

spaces, as often used to store household clutter as to park cars. The problem, of course, is what to do with the clutter (or with the car). One solution is to add on—either at the side, the rear, or above.

As part of the remodel of their 1960s California ranch house, architects Kurt Lavenson and Lesly Avedisian converted an existing freestanding garage into a workplace for their design business. The old garage, which was used primarily as a toolshed, occupied the prime spot on their property under the sweeping canopy of a 300-year-old oak tree. They needed an office at home that was removed from the

## Garage Comfort

Converting a garage to office space typically involves a considerable amount of construction. The garage floor is most likely an uninsulated concrete slab (which can be extremely cold during the winter) that slopes slightly toward the overhead door. You can solve the insulation and leveling problems at the same time by constructing a level wood frame over the existing slab and insulating the cavities below the new wood deck surface.

Also consider insulating the walls and roof of the garage and adding a heating system, which may simply bridge off your existing system or be an independent unit.

### Leveling and Insulating a Sloped Slab

Finished floor (hardwood or carpet)

1-in. (min.) rigid insulation between sleepers

Plywood subfloor

Vapor barrier

Existing sloped slab

Building paper

Fir sleepers @ 16 in. o.c. (rip as required to make level)

Note: Conditions vary. Consult with your builder or architect before construction.

◀The renovated garage features two sets of double doors, which open 180 degrees, turning the office (at right) and the pool wet room (at left) into extensions of the pool deck and garden. A stunning, 300-year-old oak tree shades much of the property.

house for privacy but at the same time maintained good visual connections and easy access to it.

Kurt and Lesly gutted the building and reconfigured the overhead garage doors for wood-framed glass doors. They constructed a small tower at one end to contain equipment for the nearby pool and the air-tempering equipment for the new workplace, and built a garage addition onto the back of the old one.

The original 25-ft. by 25-ft. garage was remodeled for flexible office space and a casual conference area that doubles as a small guest room. The square plan is divided into four equal quadrants, which pivot around a central 6x6 post that was added under the existing ridge beam (see the floor plan at right). Large pocket doors converge at the post and can be opened to create one large space or closed for privacy

## Garage Conversion

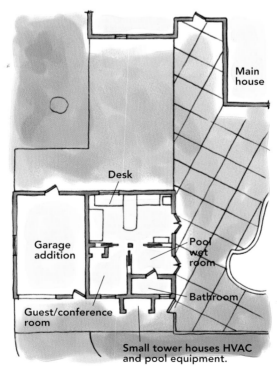

Main house

Desk

Garage addition

Pool wet room

Guest/conference room

Bathroom

Small tower houses HVAC and pool equipment.

▲ The arrangement of pocket doors around a center post allows for a variety of space configurations to accommodate changing work situations, visitors, and guests.

as necessary. The bathroom, located in the foyer, can be used for the pool, the guest room, or the office.

Desks in the office are made from birch-veneer door slabs, edged with Douglas fir and supported on file cabinets and flat files. The couple also incorporated a piece of galvanized culvert piping as the main support leg for the middle, shared desktop. ■

# Once a Toolshed, Now a Studio

**N**ever underestimate the workplace potential of any outbuilding on your property, no matter how small it is. Keith Roberts lovingly converted what was an old toolshed into this jewel of a workplace for his wife, Priscilla, who is a commercial artist.

A big part of the charm of the one-room studio is the wraparound veranda that Keith added, inspired by a lighthouse keeper's house that he'd seen on Key West. Windows and doors were either recycled from old buildings or donated by friends. The corrugated, galvanized tin roof cost a bit more to install, but it should last 50 years or more.

Keeping a house or outbuilding in the South cool in summer can be a challenge—especially if you don't want to use air conditioning. Keith took full advantage of the existing toolshed's location (on a marsh on

▲ Double French doors, leftovers from another building long since renovated, provide light and spacious entry to the studio, which has two workstations.

◀ It's hard to imagine that this beautifully crafted one-room art studio was once a simple toolshed with no veranda.

the intracoastal waterway in northern Florida), elevating the building a couple of feet and using awning windows to allow marsh breezes to pass beneath and through the studio. A vented attic with ridge vent creates a "chimney" effect, aided by a ceiling-mounted paddle-wheel fan. The Spanish tile floor, set on concrete board, stays cool during the sultry summer months. The studio is well insulated and needs only a small space heater to keep it warm during the cooler months.

▲Working at home has its virtues, but with a view as captivating as this it can be tough to get any work done.

◄The corner workstation gets cross breezes from the old-style, aluminum-framed awning windows.

◄The little garage studio is nestled in the trees just a short walk from the main house. Entry to the studio is unannounced, around back.

## Weaver's Workplace

More modest in scale than the previous example, Don and Betty Lou's garage studio is another conversion of an existing outbuilding—in this case achieved without adding square footage. When the couple purchased their 1930s-vintage Connecticut home, the property already had a detached garage with an unheated, uninsulated room above, which was albeit in a sad state of repair due to damage from the weather and several generations of raccoons. In spite of the damage, Don saw the possibilities of the room, which cantilevers over the garage on both sides to create an 18-ft.-square floor area, and set about restoring it as a studio for wife Betty Lou, who is a weaver and craftswoman.

Like the main house, the garage is set on a fieldstone foundation. Don gutted the interior to the frame, made

◄▼At the gable end of the studio overlooking the driveway, the owner set up three separate workstations. Her administrative station sits along the gable wall, illuminated by natural light from the newly introduced Palladian window above. To the right is a spinning wheel with easy chair; to the left, a drawing and project table. Supplies are neatly tucked at a kneewall corner.

repairs as necessary, added insulation, and introduced electric baseboard heat. The couple were keen to maintain the existing exposed, hand-peeled chestnut beams, and these were repaired and reshored as part of the renovation. Drywall was carefully hand-trimmed to fit between the exposed beams, conforming tightly to each curve of the timber. The original wood floor was also salvaged and restored.

The woods around the little outbuilding had grown in considerably since the garage was constructed in 1930. To compensate for the solar blockage, Don added skylights, a Palladian window, kneewall awnings, and a divided-lite

## Out the Window

Fire codes require that windows in certain rooms be of a clear minimum width and height when open, so that in the event of a fire firefighters can get in and get the occupants out. Bedrooms that are being converted to workplaces should already be in compliance. If you're converting attic or basement space or renovating an outbuilding, local building and/or fire codes may require you to add, enlarge, or reconfigure at least one window in order to ensure safe egress in the event of a fire.

◄Don set up a work area for himself to the left of the entry door, with storage and counter surface strategically occupying the low-headroom kneewall area.

▼Betty Lou has her loom in a corner to the right of the entry door. Operable awning windows feed cross-ventilation in the warmer weather, while the skylight above provides ample natural light.

door. The resulting space is now awash with light and natural ventilation.

Entry to the cozy little workplace is at the rear of the garage, up a flight of stairs and onto a small deck. On the inside, the couple were able to set up five distinct work-station zones: an administrative station, spinning wheel, loom, and drawing table for Betty Lou; and a desk/computer station in the corner for husband Don, who works as a home-based insurance agent. Quite an achievement in a one-room workplace of barely 300 sq. ft. ■

►Computer and music stations are well integrated for the owner's audiovisual work. The keyboard occupies the exact center of the second-story space.

▲The renovation and second-story addition to the existing garage are in keeping with the style of the main house, pictured in the background.

## A Signature Music Studio

One of the five basic tenets of successful home-workplace planning that I outlined in chapter 1 is that you should design a place for *who you are*. This converted garage workplace in Newton, Massachusetts, is a great example of a homeowner who has done just that.

The owner is an audiovisual artist who provides both graphic design and soundtracks for TV shows and also makes commercials for local television stations. Originally working out of his house, he converted a ramshackle, one-story garage into a magnificent two-story, carriage-style outbuilding, with garage space maintained on the lower level and workplace above.

The first step was to consult with architect Malcolm MacKenzie, who worked with the owner to conceptualize

## Second-Floor Music Studio

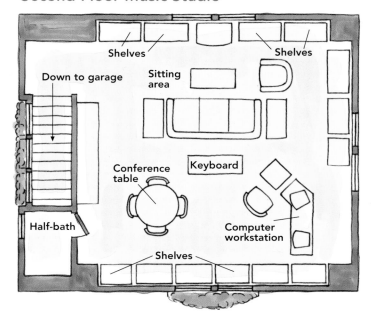

the building as well as to orchestrate the town approval process (see the sidebar at right). The owner wanted a simple, open space within which he could arrange his project stations (one of which is a Kurzweil keyboard) and have a comfortable seating area. The architect and owner agreed that the new building's design should draw inspiration from the existing house, a turn-of-the-century, shingle-style affair, with crossing gambrel roofs and lots of windows. The owner also wanted a place to display and enjoy his significant collection of antique American signs, which became part of the overall program.

MacKenzie replicated the double-cross gambrel roof of the main house, but with one difference—it was entirely open from within. Exposed flying beams tie the walls together, compensating for lateral thrust from the roof loads. Another special feature is the stepped array of windows at the gable end. Skylights within the roof and windows on all four sides provide abundant light, the bright walls and vaulted ceiling serving as perfect backdrops for the owner's sign collection.

# An Exception to the Rule

No matter how well meaning, local building regulations can sometimes be financially burden-some. If the case is justifiable and presented properly, a local building authority just might be willing to make an exception.

That's what happened in the case of the music studio featured here. The owner wanted to include a half-bath in the work space. Regulations in the town where he lives require that if a new rest room of any kind is constructed in an outbuilding, it has to be connected directly to the main waste line in the road, not simply run back to the house. The architect determined this would multiply the costs of the project fourfold.

After discussions with the town, it became apparent that the real issue was the town's concern that the owner might eventually convert the workplace to a separate dwelling unit. This concern was overcome by the owner's agreeing to sign a statement-of-purpose affidavit. The conversion was then approved as an accessory work space with the less expensive plumbing solution.

▲Away from the workstations, a casual sitting area is a place to relax, catch up on the news, and enjoy the owner's impressive collection of American signs.

Artificial ambient lighting is in the style of the Craftsman era, which is the period in which many of the signs were fabricated and in popular commercial use. Four fixtures are ceiling mounted on pendants, blending in perfectly with the decor, while task light is provided by period lamps at sitting height. One final feature of note is the storage, which consists of industrial shelving units that run around the perimeter of the room. Units are kept low so that the view from the windows is not obscured. ■

## Carriage-Barn Conversion

Here's one final take on the converted out-building theme, once again with a second-floor workplace, though this time in a carriage barn, not a garage. With a busy, home-based, architectural practice and a growing family, Susan Snell had outgrown the office in the front room of her upstate New York home. A carriage barn behind the 19th-century home offered the perfect opportunity to be out of the house, but not too far away.

The ground floor of the converted barn serves as a meeting and model-building area, with a bay set aside for yard storage concealed behind the original barn doors. The upper level, under the gabled roof, became the main production area, with a continuous counter space running around three sides and connecting the two workstations (see the floor plan at right).

What could have been a fairly unexceptional space has been transformed into a studio of distinction by the judicious use of color, lighting, finish materials, and attention to detail. The ceiling is clad with natural-finish 1x4 Douglas fir boards;

▲The ground floor serves as a meeting room and general project layout space.

## Second-Floor Architect's Studio

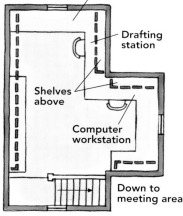

**Continuous counter space continues more thatn halfway around the perimeter walls.**

Drafting station

Shelves above

Computer workstation

Down to meeting area

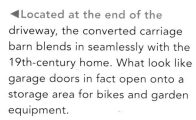

◀Located at the end of the driveway, the converted carriage barn blends in seamlessly with the 19th-century home. What look like garage doors in fact open onto a storage area for bikes and garden equipment.

painted collar ties, cut to form a simple arc, add further character. Susan repeated the arc motif in the window heads and at the ends of custom-crafted bookcases, and designed a simple board-and-batten treatment for the gable-end walls.

Fluorescent-strip, under-cabinet lighting supplements natural light and provides even illumination for desktop work. Industrial-type incandescent brackets light the upper areas of the studio. Thinking ahead, Susan planned the office to be easily convertible to a guest house, for purposes of eventual resale. ■

▲ In the second-floor studio, counters along the perimeter wall combined with shelving placed high on the kneewall provide abundant work-surface and storage space.

▶ Arched collar ties and the matching arc over the window head, along with careful use of color and finish materials, transform a second-story shell into a home workplace filled with character.

# Painting Poolside

Sally, a professional artist, has always had a work space in her home, but it wasn't until she and her husband moved to Burlington, Vermont, when the kids were older that she was able to create her dream studio outside the home. The new property had an old coach house on it, and Sally decided it was the perfect spot for her painting studio.

The lower level was kept as a garage, but, working with her contractor, Sally raised the roof and added large windows

◀Landscaping conceived as part of the overall studio plan creates the atmosphere of a "secret garden" pathway.

▼The pool aligns perfectly with the studio, providing a serene and meditative view from above.

◀ Raising the roof of the coach house gave Sally all the room she needs in the upstairs studio to work on her large paintings.

▼ Built-in shelving frames a picture window and creates a window seat. The window displays artifacts that are important to Sally and to her work.

that match the style of the main house. The most striking design feature is the balcony, an elliptical shape that mimics the eyebrow window and visually extends the studio beyond the walls of the coach house. Outside the building, Sally developed a "secret garden" landscape scheme and added a long, narrow swimming pool that aligns axially with the main elevation of the new studio.

The upper studio interior, approximately 20 ft. square, is totally open space, with a small bathroom in one corner. Even though the footprint is modest, the high-peaked ceiling allows the painter to "work large." The wide doorway to the balcony provides an exit route for her largest works, which can be hoisted down to ground level. Southern and western exposures are almost totally glazed, filling the studio with natural light.

# New Construction: Crafting a New Vessel

If there's a final frontier in the world of the home workplace, it's the construction of a dedicated outbuilding on raw land. But before you get carried away with the dream of building a workplace from scratch in your own backyard, you need to weigh all the practical considerations that are involved.

Site engineering becomes a priority with a new building. Issues of waste water, power connections, parking, and drainage will all have to be worked through, along with standard issues such as setback requirements and floor-area to lot-area ratios. Two buildings on one lot are an automatic "let's see what's going on here"

▲ **The owners of this North Carolina home** took their design inspiration from classic Japanese architecture and included a workplace that stands apart from the home but at the same time is connected to it by an elegant, terraced breezeway.

◄ **The workplace is simply furnished**, with an elegant wood slab as the main workstation, served by a matching pedestal drawer unit. A small bathroom and kitchen at the back of the studio permit the couple to convert the workplace to guest quarters as needed.

# Office to Go

If hiring an architect to design a custom building is beyond your budget, an alternative is to work with a company that makes prefabricated buildings. Post-and-beam structures and log cabins are popular choices, but there are also a number of companies that produce more modest, portable workplaces for sale or lease.

One of these companies is Soho2go of Jericho, Vermont, which produces a range of modular home offices that are available as a kit or preassembled and delivered. The one-room buildings feature state-of-the-art structural insulated panel (SIP) construction and raceways for flexible power and communications connections. Simply plug in the power, hook up the telephone and modem, and you've got a fully functioning home workplace in your own backyard.

◄A portable, modular building is a cost-effective way to obtain a place of your own. To avoid a closed-in feeling, this unit has double sliding doors instead of a standard door.

▲The interior vaulted ceiling makes the modest workplace feel a little more spacious.

to most building authorities. Some towns might flat-out refuse to issue a permit for a second building, so don't get too far along until you've checked out all the particulars (including cost). That said, you do already own the land, and there are many modest ways to develop a small, new workplace building, whether it be custom-built or delivered on a truck bed (see the sidebar above). ■

# A Studio Afloat
# in the Woods

When professional artist Sheila Blake sets out for work in the morning, she steps out onto the rear deck of her bungalow-style home, follows a carefully proportioned wooden walkway through the backyard, and walks into a different world. The delicately sited backyard pavilion that architect Travis Price designed for her is all that she ever wanted: a special place that stimulates her creativity in a location that marks a distinct separation between work and home.

Entry to the copper-sided studio is at the rear end of the building, which may seem opposite to what you'd expect. But this arrangement allows the double-corner slid-

▲ The owner's deep, gently sloping, and attractively wooded rear yard is the perfect location for her art studio. The entry faces away from the house and into the woods, ensuring privacy and a distinct separation between work and home.

ing doors to frame a view of nature rather than look back at the living quarters, further reinforcing the separation between work and home. The building is supported by exposed concrete piers, which was economical because it eliminated the need for a foundation and also saved a few trees from being destroyed by excavation. The effect is of a building floating above its natural surrounds.

Inside the studio, the most striking feature is the band of fixed glass that runs between the structural wall members at floor level. This unusual detail allows almost all the interior wall surface to be used for exhibiting artwork, uninterrupted by windows except for a small portal near the artist's work area. The perimeter footlight

▲ The baseline perimeter band of glass brings light into the studio at floor level and frees up the walls for artwork.

## Walkway to Work

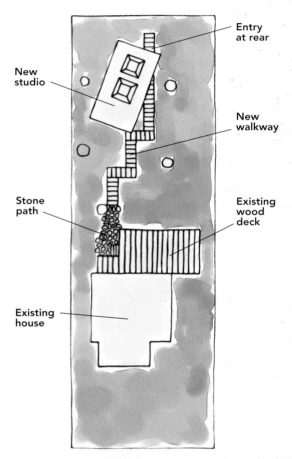

Entry at rear

New studio

New walkway

Stone path

Existing wood deck

Existing house

▲ Skylights set high into the ceiling light wells disperse natural light evenly throughout the interior of the office. The finishes are simple: a deck-painted plywood floor, fiberboard walls, and drywall ceiling.

intensifies the experience of feeling afloat, while also allowing the artist to have constant visual contact with the ground around the building. Since the eye is drawn to the light at the floor and focuses at a point outside the wall plane, the small, 300-sq.-ft. space is experienced as being much larger.

▲ A wharflike walkway leads to the studio, which seems to float above its moorings. The curved roof and skylight stacks add to the visual metaphor.

◄With matching siding and windows, the new studio (at rear) and original house complement each other nicely.

▼The entry to the studio is designed to be weather-protected, yet open and inviting.

## The Art of the Mountain Workplace

When Robin and her husband built a small house on a three-acre lot in the hills of Blacksburg, Virginia, she was delighted to have a corner where she could do her artwork. But, inevitably, she needed more space, so they decided to build a studio outbuilding about 20 ft. from the house, where Robin could paint and teach occasional classes.

The basic plan called for the studio to be above a two-car garage, dug into a steep hill. Robin originally planned connecting stairs for the two levels to be on the inside, but architect Orin Arvold suggested an external covered staircase, which saved interior space and money. He also suggested that the couple put a loft in the gable roof.

The 800-sq.-ft. studio is a variation on the theme of the original house, with cypress siding and Dry-Vit stucco work.

▲At the rear of the studio, a storage closet overhangs one bay of the garage, while a narrow window allows northern light in over the work area. The overall arrangement buffers the wall from the north wind.

Because the property is located outside town limits and Robin has no employees, she was not required to file permits for a business facility. Visitor parking was solved by a two-tiered parking area—one at the road and the other farther up the hill at house level.

As do most artists, Robin wanted lots of light, which was provided by large expanses of south-facing glass and skylights. Northern windows were minimized, introduced only at task locations for the benefit of northern light. The interior is mostly open for freedom of movement and flexibility. A centrally located woodstove keeps the space toasty warm,

▲A vaulted ceiling (with lofts tucked within) enlarges the studio space. The spiral stair and wood-burning stove are attractive, practical features.

◄Large, south-facing windows and skylights allow light to pour in. Thermal brick on the southern floor absorbs heat and moderates temperature changes.

while electrical baseboard heat is used as a backup. To maximize on heat from the sun, the floor on the southern half of the studio was finished with 4-in. thermal brick, which acts as a heat sink and helps moderate temperature fluctuations.

A large closet stores assorted clutter—paint materials, unframed paintings of various sizes, art supplies, and so on. The loft is accessed by a spiral stair, which conserves floor space. The loft has a computer station and also doubles as a guest room. An additional bunk-bed loft—perfect for visiting kids—is accessed by a ladder. The small kitchen and bath allow Robin the flexibility to occasionally turn the whole studio over to short-stay visitors, affording them total privacy from the main house. (See the sidebar at right for more on plumbing.) ■

## Need Plumbing?

If you're planning on adding a sink to your home workplace, you'll have to be concerned with the delivery of hot and cold water, the removal of waste water, and ventilating of the waste line. Plumbing can affect other aspects of the house because lines and stacks take up space and often require the opening of walls or ceilings. If your existing hot water heater is far away from the new sink location, you may want to consider putting in a smaller, separate hot water heater at the new location.

If you are planning on adding a rest room, the large-diameter waste line for the toilet is the most difficult line to run. As a rule, the closer you can position the new wet areas to existing water and waste lines, the less difficult and costly it will be to install them.

▲A floating wood-strip floor over a poured concrete slab on grade covers the 100-sq.-ft. seating area, with guitars, records, and recording/listening equipment tucked into cantilevered bays.

►Connected to the main house via a wood deck, the little music shed sits among the trees and shrubs of the beautifully landscaped rear yard.

## A One-Man Music Shed

Tom and Diane own a small cottage in San Francisco. Tom, who is in the music business, initially wanted to add a room onto the house where he could work on musical compositions, listen to music, and store his large collection of albums, guitars, and Beatles memorabilia. When Tom called architect John Rohosky to see about an addition, he quickly learned that there was no room to build out on the tight urban lot and that a second-floor addition would require a total, and very expensive, seismic retrofit.

Architect Rohosky did some code research and found that there was enough room to build a small garden shed, which could also be used as a music room or storage facility. But there was a limit on size— the footprint couldn't exceed 10 ft. by 10 ft. Rohosky cleverly got around the size limitation by designing cantilevered storage and equipment bays on three sides. The bays would hold albums, guitars, and recording equipment, while the 10 ft. by 10 ft. footprint would be open space for seating (see the floor plan on p. 196). The cantilevered bays were legal because they weren't considered part of the footprint, yet they expand the effective area of the shed by more than 40 percent. The

◀The nicely detailed exposed-roof structure brings the eye upward toward the skylight cap, a trick that expands the perceived size of the space.

## Music Studio with Cantilevered Bays

Equipment bay

Storage bay

Fixed window

Pyramidal skylight above

Storage bay

Hopper window

Hopper window

French doors open to deck toward main house.

bays step up a bit at the ground level, which is helpful in the case of storage because it keeps things from being too low to the floor.

The new outbuilding opens onto a small wood deck that connects to the main house. With doors open, the deck becomes an extension of the shed and the house as well. With doors closed, Tom can work on compositions without disturbing anyone in the house.

To avoid a closed-in feeling in the relatively small space, Rohosky designed an attractive exposed-beam roof structure, capped by a pyramidal fixed skylight. Flow-through ventilation is achieved by small hopper windows above the two storage bays and an additional venting skylight on the back side of the roof. The roof deck is also ventilated within, using a system of breathing strips and ridge vents so air can flow through and over the batt insulation within the roof sandwich. ■

## Combining Work and Play

Here's another excellent example of an artisan who has designed a workplace that reflects his unique personal spirit. Andre Harvey is an internationally acclaimed sculptor who is best known for the life-size animal works that he casts in bronze. When he and his wife, Bobbie, began planning a new home in Delaware, they knew exactly what they wanted: a house that reflected the enduring gray stone, cottage-style architecture of the surrounding Brandywine River Valley; and a dedicated outbuilding where Andre could work and pursue his passion for collecting automobilia. The resulting barn studio and residence, designed by architect John Milner and built in 1990, could easily pass for a perfectly restored mid-19th-century farmstead.

▼At first glance, the buildings look as though they've been comfortably nestled into the land for a hundred years or more. Both house and barn studio were constructed in 1990.

◀Double doors at the main wing of the barn allow for movement of the owner's large sculptural pieces—or a restored tractor—in and out of the studio.

Beyond the design aesthetic, the studio outbuilding had to satisfy two major functional requirements. First, Andre needed a place to design, construct, and display his sculptural work, which varies dramatically in size; his art ranges from small, jewelry-size pieces to the large bronze castings pictured at right. Second, he wanted a place to store and display his sizable automotive collection, which includes early farm vehicles.

The barn is made up of two connected sections. The main portion is where Andre conceptualizes his sculptural creations and does finish work, especially on the smaller, jewelry pieces. Workbenches and layout tables coexist with advertising signs, antique garage tools, and a perfectly restored tractor. A balcony level beneath the open vaulted ceiling is used mainly for storing additional pieces of the collection.

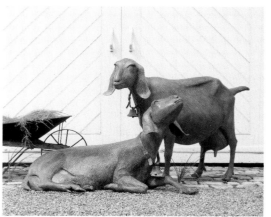

▲The sculptor is best known for his life-size, bronze animal castings, two of which are shown here at the double-door entry to the studio.

The second, attached part of the building section has a lower roof and is dedicated to heavier work, such as welding, sandblasting, and sawing. This area can be isolated from the main studio and separately ventilated to prevent dust, fumes, and other heavy work by-products from migrating into the main wing of the studio.

While Andre's work and personal interests are unique to him, his studio exemplifies the three key features of any good home workplace: a balance of home and work life, a place that is well planned and organized, and a personal spirit that's a reflection of its owner. ■

▼ Looking from the balcony onto the main studio floor, it's hard to tell where the work stops and the hobby begins.

# A Writer's Retreat

▲ This small jewel of a writer's retreat, with dramatic river overlooks, is accessed by a short bridge.

Architect James Stageburg designed this tiny retreat for his wife, Susan, who is a writer. Husband and wife work at home quite a lot, and they found that their weekend cottage just didn't afford Susan the privacy she requires. James likes to whistle and sing while he works; Susan likes the stone silence of a tomb.

The couple's 5-acre property in Wisconsin overlooks the Mississippi River. James hunted around to find a good view from a reasonably buildable spot on the steep ridge, which towers 500 ft. above the river. The exterior is covered in shingles that are stained in various shades of green; a wood bridge, trimmed in red and purple, bounds over the bluff to meet the entry. The barreled roof reads inside and out, covered on

**Writer's Retreat**

Stairs down to studio

Entry bridge from cottage

the interior with beadboard. A band of windows poke out over the view on the curved front wall, while a triangular slice lodged beneath the barrel roof floods the room with natural light.

▲ The writer's requirements were minimal—a counter where she could work, a daybed, heat, electricity, and, most important of all, quiet.

## Office in a Tree House

This chapter has showcased some unique home workplaces, but for originality it's tough to beat the treetop workplace that homebuilder John Rouches constructed for himself in Washington state. John's business partner, Peter Nelson, enjoys a national reputation as a tree-house design expert, and after Peter built himself a home-office crow's nest in the trees, John decided he had to have one too.

A tree house has certain advantages over a land-built structure, if you don't mind a modest climb. There's no excavation, no foundation, and no piers to build, and the building and its occupants enjoy a connection with nature that's tough to match on the ground. John's tree-house workplace sits on a platform that, with the exception of one corner, is supported by standing trees. Built on the side of a hill, the entry end of the platform is four steps up from grade. On the downward side, the steep slope parts 14 ft. away from the underside of the platform, which provides a perch for the tree house and its commanding view. Electricity (for heat, light, and power) runs underground and up one of the trees, in conduit to a panel within the tree house. Phone lines and cable run within the same conduit.

The interior plan, in 175 sq. ft. of heated space, was a co-operative effort between John's wife, Inga, and friend and interior designer Sally Owen. Planned for dual use as a guest house and a workplace, a countertop work area folds up and

▲ The tree house sits on a platform that is undergirded into four equally sized cedar trees—one at the corner entry area of the steps, and three behind. The trunks remain fully outside the cabin.

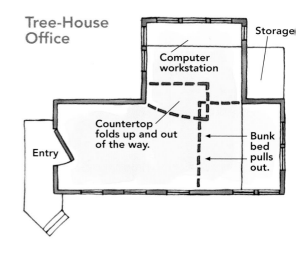

**Tree-House Office**

Storage

Computer workstation

Countertop folds up and out of the way.

Entry

Bunk bed pulls out.

▲The workplace is tucked into an "ell" with a dormered shed roof. An outer-counter leaf serves as lay space and a meeting table. Hinged at the wall, it can be lifted up and out of the way for expanded floor space.

▼A bunk bed at the gable end is expandable to queen size when the tree house is pressed into service as a guest house. Interior finishes are exposed, paint-stained plywood and recycled fir boards.

out of the way. A bunk over storage bins pulls out to become a full-size bed (see the floor plan on the facing page).

John is an avid sailor, so Sally suggested that they introduce a nautical theme, using a variety of parts either bought at marine salvage or provided by John. A tree house is in many ways like a boat, John explains, because of the efficiencies required by tight quarters and dual functions. Also not unlike a boat, it rides aloft within an ever-changing natural element, affected by wind and the continued change of its bearings. No one ever said working at home couldn't be a daily adventure. ■

# Going Public

►If you build it, they will come. Opening up your home workplace to the public introduces a whole new set of issues to consider, including parking, accessibility, and signage.

I n our final chapter, we'll look at workplaces where visitors are expected on a regular basis—workplaces that greet the public. While "going public" workplaces have some unique requirements, it's worth repeating that they must still embody the three basic principles of good home-workplace design: They balance home and work life, they're well planned and organized, and they have a personal spirit about them.

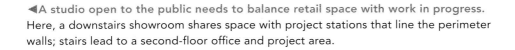

In going public, however, the separation between home and work life involves a higher-level plan for separating the public from what is private. This is most commonly (although not always) accomplished by developing a workplace in an outbuilding. With a stand-alone building, not only is the workplace isolated from the living space, but the physical approach is as

◄A studio open to the public needs to balance retail space with work in progress. Here, a downstairs showroom shares space with project stations that line the perimeter walls; stairs lead to a second-floor office and project area.

◀A meeting area is often a key requirement for a "public" workplace. Here, an architect's office in a garage provides a separate and a comfortable sitting area for meeting with clients.

well. This makes for a clear distinction to the visitor, and interruptions of home life are far less likely to occur.

Second, organization is very important because the workplace is now seen by the public. Organization counts for more than neatness in a public situation—it also has to do with safety. Paths of egress, fire hazards, aisle-way widths, and accessibility now become concerns of local building authorities. Finally, a workplace that reflects the personality of its occupant now conveys that message to visitors. That message, embedded within the environment, is the single most important advertisement for customers or clients who visit the home-based workplace or business. ▪

◀▼When home workplaces host employees or invite the public, it's important that areas in public view be kept organized and tidy. Production areas that are neat, spacious, bright, and open make an excellent first impression.

# Getting Approval

Aworkplace that proposes to invite the public also invites closer scrutiny from the officials who are empowered with the responsibility to approve or deny the request. It's not unusual for a public hearing to be scheduled to review a proposal. Let's take a brief look at the factors that are typically involved in the approvals process.

Before any plans are drawn, local authorities will want to know some details about your proposed workplace activity, generally referred to as "occupancy use." Most towns have maps that subdivide the town into zones, which permit and restrict various uses. This prevents, for example, factories from being constructed next to single-family residences.

▼Workplaces that receive visitors should be as welcoming as possible. In this beautiful home workplace, the meeting area in the foreground is homey, warm, and casual, yet still very professional.

## Accessibility

Accessible design is a concern in any workplace, but particularly in locations that are visited by the public. Regulations governing handicap accessibility are found within building codes and the Americans with Disabilities Act. Some states have created independent "access review" boards, which are authorized by law to review and approve plans solely for accessibility as a prerequisite to filing for a building permit.

At minimum, workplaces that serve the public require accessible parking, a code-conforming access ramp if entry is not at grade, and accessible rest-room facilities. In addition, certain other accessibility regulations may apply to your particular business and building layout. It's wise to check with local building authorities about accessibility issues in the initial pre-planning stage, and then to have plans developed by someone who is thoroughly familiar with accessibility issues governing public places within your building jurisdiction.

▲Although this workplace is newly built, it was planned for flexibility, so that future owners could convert it to a garage. The first-floor space is currently used as a meeting room for an at-home architects' business.

Generally speaking, the more rural your location, and the more separated you are from your neighbors, the more likely it is you will be able to obtain approval. The bottom line is that you can't just "go public" without permission to proceed. There are no universal rules, but an easy way to test the waters is to make an appointment with a building official and talk about your plans.

Assuming you haven't run into an immediate red flag, the town will also be concerned about your property and how neighbors might be affected by activities that create traffic, vehicular and/or pedestrian. At this point, the town will probably want to see a preliminary plan—a scaled drawing that indicates the location and size of the workplace, entrances and exits, and its position relative to surveyed property lines. Even if you are properly zoned for a specific

▲The storefront glass at the conference area can be protected by storm doors. Double doors in the second-floor work space open onto a viewing deck. Both rooms face eastern views of the Atlantic Ocean.

◀Upstairs, the studio is furnished with matching his-and-hers drawing tables and computer stations on opposite walls.

## Site Plan

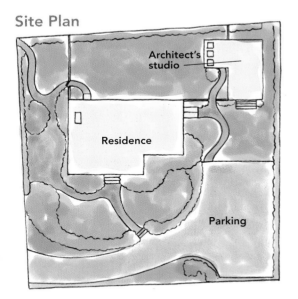

Architect's studio

Residence

Parking

existing house and its surrounds. Detailing and materials selection were therefore very much in keeping with the traditional building style of the area. Construction from entirely new materials would have been simpler and less costly, but the couple managed to locate antique Douglas fir beams and structural decking, salvaged from the demolition of an old high-school auditorium. The recycled materials are left exposed as interior finish for the first- and second-floor beamed-and-trussed ceilings. Walls were framed conventionally but covered with plasterboard and finished with veneer-plaster, then painted.

David says, "I know I'd never find a more pleasant space in which to work while so close and convenient to home." Most of us would be hard-pressed to disagree. ■

## A Decoy Maker Carves a Niche

Gary carved his first decoy when he was nine years old, but it wasn't until 1987, after a successful career in the food-service industry, that he decided to turn his personal passion into a full-time business venture. For 12 years, he carved and painted in the basement of the 1840 farmhouse that he shares with wife Kathy. Over time, he developed a significant word-of-mouth and mail-order clientele, and the couple decided to construct a new outbuilding studio for the now-proven business.

The property rests within a community of old dairy farms, and the plan was to move an existing two-car garage to a location farther back in the property and replace it with the studio on an enlarged foundation. The town of Weybridge, Vermont, approved Gary's preliminary plans at the first zoning-board meeting. Since there would be no business signs by the road—visits are by appointment only—traffic and parking were not serious issues.

Gary wanted the new outbuilding to blend in with the architectural style of his neighbors' farm and barn buildings, as well as that of his own 1840 Cape-style house. He was able to acquire a post-and-beam frame structure that was salvaged from a hundred-year-old barn, and he used it as a starting point for the design, with minor reconfigurations to the original frame.

▲ Entry to the studio and showroom is through an antique triple-Dutch door, with fixed bottom leaves that now act together. The topmost section is a fixed transom.

The new footprint is about 800 sq. ft., with a total height of 30 ft. to the peak, and an atrium that penetrates full-through to ground level. The first floor provides space for the retail store, the main woodwork areas, and raw inventory storage. The second floor contains the working office—computers, shipping and packing, and a painting area, along with a library and completed inventory storage area—and a rest room. The third floor, which is occasionally used as an observatory, has open-grid flooring that allows light to penetrate into the atrium.

Traditional building themes were showcased wherever possible. Gary used a composite panel system to enclose the structure, so that the post-and-beam frame would be exposed on the inside. He found a remnant triple Dutch door

► The decoy-surrounded owner in the second-floor work area. The exposed, antique post-and-beam structure is a perfect visual backdrop for his hand-crafted creations.

◀The gridded floor on the third level is accessed by a ladder from level two. The windowed cupola not only allows light into the atrium through the gridded floor, but also makes an excellent observatory.

from a long-gone nearby cavalry building, and modified it for use as the main entry door to the studio. For exterior cladding, he used raw pine rough-cut from a local sawmill. It was applied in a time-worn reverse board-and-batten assembly, which allows the raw lumber to shrink and season without splitting.

One place Gary broke with tradition was in his choice of heating system, opting for radiant hot-water heat, which is a wise choice for a building whose main floor is on a slab-at-grade in cold climate. A little closet on the ground floor holds pumping and zoning equipment for the heat system, which receives hot water from the boiler in the basement of the main house.

Overall, the design of the new building is supportive of Gary's work in several ways. From a functional point of view, it gives him the space and light he needs. From an aesthetic point of view, it blends in beautifully with the community, which is always a plus for neighborly relations. But beyond that, the design concept is in harmony with his traditional wood handiwork business, and therefore acts as an ideal backdrop. ■

## Salvaged Materials

As you plan your own home workplace, you may want to consider using salvaged materials. There are two main benefits: First, you can build a certain old-world charm into what may be an otherwise high-tech environment, and, second, there may be a considerable cost savings.

Salvaged building materials include everything from beams and roofing materials to windows and doors. You might also find a place in your workspace for salvaged wainscoting, interior light fixtures (especially ambient pendant mount), and antique furniture, all of which can often be purchased at a reasonable cost. The re-use of these materials adds warmth, interest, and personality to your work nest.

▲The artist stands proudly within the double doorway of her new workplace, which was formerly a three-car garage.

## A Garage Becomes a Teaching Studio

When you make the step up from working alone to going public, you'll probably find that you have to rethink the place where you work. For Carol, a Vermont artist and educator, the move was from a cramped basement workplace to a three-car garage, which she converted into a painting, printing, and teaching studio.

Before beginning the design, Carol identified three space requirements. First, she wanted a space where she could work on large paintings in an area that would not be disturbed or moved when groups came in. Second, she wanted

▶The teaching area is surrounded by well-organized supply storage, which is readily accessible. An etching press (behind) is one of the many interesting features within the new workplace.

▲A vaulted area in one of the bays provides ample space for the owner to work on large images. Natural light comes in from above, thereby preserving the wall for painting. Floodlights in recessed ceiling fixtures provide general illumination, with adjustable spot and highlight lighting from track lighting along the bottom of exposed overhead tie beams.

a teaching space that could accommodate ten children or six adults. And last, she wanted what she refers to as a "green" space, or a sitting area where she could read, make notes, and hold meetings for her women-artists' group (see the floor plan on the facing page).

When Carol paid a visit to the local planning board, the members determined that since she'd been running classes from the basement of her home for several years, there was no need to go before a more formal planning commission. They felt that the groups were small enough that it wasn't an issue, and she already had plenty of on-site parking.

The building was a standard three-bay garage, with no heat, insulation, finishes, or adequate power. All this would have to be introduced in order to make the garage habitable

► The comfortable sitting area is a great spot from which to enjoy the river view through casement windows. Storage for a variety of different-size books, paintings, and CDs is built into an alcove behind the sitting area. Art of longer dimensions penetrates through the wall into the closet/storage area behind.

## Artist's Studio

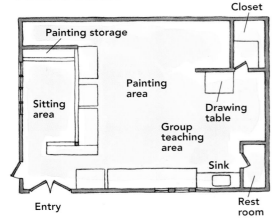

as a studio (a new power service and a water line were brought in from the main house). In addition, the existing slab floor had to be framed with wood, leveled, insulated with rigid board, and covered with plywood (see the drawing on p. 173). The garage doors were removed, the wall in-filled, and double glass entry doors introduced into one of the existing bays, looking back toward the house.

Carol wanted to get as much light as possible into the building but also maintain wall space. Large casement windows on the southwest wall, the glass expanse at the river-view sitting area, and the glass double doors bring plenty of natural light into the space. Windows at the peak of the southeast side of the building bring in morning light over-head into the vaulted ceiling area, but stay clear of the wall below where Carol works. ■

# Working Out at Home

For Karen and Lou, a change in family circumstances was the impetus to create a very special home-based business. Karen owned and operated an aerobics studio in rental space about 10 miles from their home. When she gave birth to daughter Sara Jo, who was diagnosed with cerebral palsy and would require ongoing care, Karen's daily work routine had to change. The couple had previously toyed with the idea of building a fitness studio for Karen behind their house, but now the need was pressing.

Karen's main building requirement was for a large open space with clear spans. Taking his inspiration from gothic architec-ture, Lou came up with a simple plan for a 28-ft.-by-40-ft. stone building with a high roofline. Guests would arrive at the entry door, with changing and rest rooms

▲ The aerobics studio is housed in a newly constructed stone outbuilding inspired by Gothic architecture.

◀ Inside, the studio is one large workout space, with a changing room (left) and bathroom (right) flanking the entry and bank of windows. Stairs lead to a mezzanine-level loft.

adjacent. Beyond these utility spaces, the exercise area would open up into a clear-span space with a cathedral ceiling. A mezzanine over the utility spaces would be used for storage and ancillary space. Karen could do the administrative chores at home, closer to Sara Jo. She loved what she saw, and without much further ado, the couple paid a visit to the local building department.

In their rural New Hampshire town, the zoning board's main concern was how adjacent neighbors would be affected. Fortunately, their 150-acre land parcel was a natural buffer; in addition, parking was adequate and there was no need for any signage. The building officials were satisfied and granted a permit.

Lou, a self-employed masonry contractor, did much of the construction himself, saving money by buying materials directly from area mills (including good-quality "seconds" at steep discounts) and windows at a construction-yard sale. One of the key features of an aerobics studio is a comfortable floor with a springy quality that lowers impact during workouts. The building sits on a slab, over which Lou built a suspended ash wood floor that floats over special padding on 2x4 sleepers. Insulation between sleepers maintains an even temperature at the floor as well. A kerosene-fired heating system blows warm air into the open space.

In the seven years since the building has been open, the studio has grown into a gathering place and has become an integral part of local community life. People come as much for the environment, the gardens, and the socializing as they do for the courses. Karen now conducts 15 classes per week, with a regular membership of 80. Additional instructors teach classes in ballroom and country dancing and yoga, and the space is rented out for various workshops.

Karen says that, if not for Sara Jo, all of this would never have happened, and she adds, "Sara Jo has had a profoundly positive effect on our lives and those she touches within our community. We count ourselves very lucky."

▲ More than just a place to work out, the studio has become an integral part of local community life.

▲The studio pavilion,
a study in sculpted planes,
sits majestically over a reflective pond.

## At Work in a Glass Pavilion

We've come a long way on our work-at-home journey, and this spectacular contemporary addition is an inspiring place to end. At 1,200 sq. ft., it's a far cry from a makeshift office at the kitchen table, but like any successful home workplace it reflects the unique personality of its owners.

Architect Mark Dziewulski designed the pavilion addition for a couple who wanted a finely sculpted office and studio attachment to their northern California home. In addition to providing work space, the pavilion houses their art collection and is occasionally used for gatherings and charitable fund-raising events. For themselves, the owners wished to create a tranquil and sheltered environment from which to enjoy the lush landscape and spectacular water views while they work.

A steel-and-glass box can have a tendency to be "stand-offish" when it comes to its relationship with the site. Dziewulski's design is clearly ultramodern, but nevertheless he managed to set up an intimate dialogue between the building and its natural surrounds (see the drawing on p. 231). His complete mastery of modern and traditional building materials is evident here, blending them into a beautiful and sculptural composition that seems to have been chiseled into its location.

Viewed from the exterior, the entire structure gently and organically curves to take advantage of the river view, while the cantilevered floor extends over the man-made lake "Fallingwater" fashion. The extensive use of glass, introduced as a smooth plane that eventually transitions into a

▲ The night view highlights the crystalline box and exterior stair to pathways around the pond below.

▶ The interior is open, flexible, and uncluttered. Sawtooth glazing (to the left) is highlighted by track-mounted halogen lights, which follow the gentle curve of the building. The cabinet wall (to the right) is open to the glazing at seating height to preserve the view.

▲The custom-shaped, etched-glass work surface, which is supported by a simple column at the gathering end, imitates the curvature of the larger space. The glass floor panel at the rear door foreshadows the illusory levitating quality of the addition as viewed from the garden.

sawtooth, creates an almost crystalline cubelike enclosure, from within which the owners may simultaneously work and enjoy the idyllic view.

Structural glass panels in the floor allow the eye to penetrate the floor plane and gaze upon the water below, adding yet another dimension to the crystal-like interior. The uninterrupted floor-to-ceiling glass walls open the room up to the landscape, extending the boundaries of the interior, which is shaded by a soaring, cleaver-edged roof overhang. Circular penetrations in the roof, beginning outside and rhythmically coursing inside, bring light deep into the interior and provide a visual focus at the ceiling, which reads largely as a shooting horizontal plane. The disk penetrations further merge the exterior and interior space, which is interrupted only by a sheer plane of glass.

## A Finely Sculpted Addition

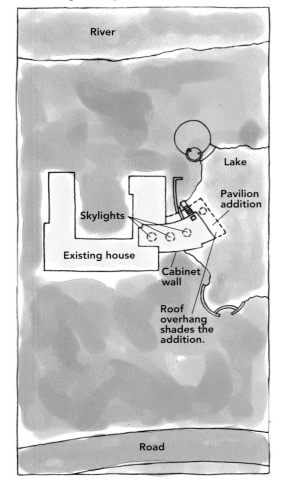

River

Lake

Pavilion addition

Skylights

Existing house

Cabinet wall

Roof overhang shades the addition.

Road

▲ A classic Eames chair adorns the outer corner, a perfect spot from which to meditate upon the magnificent pastoral view outside.

As part of the interior plan, the owners wanted a layout they could easily keep tidy and clean. The architect therefore developed a sizeable bank of cabinetry along the west wall, which would also serve to limit the penetration of western sun. The cabinetry is punctuated with slivers of window area, again breaking the box out into open space. Within the storage wall, flat files, drawings, art, and supplies all have their place, which allows the couple to keep the space clean and always ready for visitors. The resulting interior is cool, quiet, and calm, as well as a functional and aesthetic delight for its inhabitants. ■

# Credits

front cover: (top row, left) Photo © Barry Halkin; (top row, center; center row, far right; bottom row, left and right) Photos © Philip Beaurline; design: Travis Price Architects, Takoma Park, MD; (top row, right) Photo © Alan Geller; design: John Rohosky, Architecture and Construction, San Francisco, CA; (center row, far left) Photo © Michael Dunne, courtesy Elizabeth Whiting Associates, London, England; design: Andrew-Usiskin, London, England; (center row, second from left) Photo © Jamie Salomon; (center row, second from right) Photo by Charles Bickford, courtesy *Fine Homebuilding* magazine, © The Taunton Press, Inc.; design: James Stageberg, Minneapolis, MN; (bottom row, center) Photo by Charles Miller, courtesy *Fine Homebuilding* magazine, © The Taunton Press, Inc.; design: Alan Jencks, Berkeley, CA.

back cover: (top row; bottom row, second from right) Photos © Philip Beaurline; design: Travis Price Architects, Takoma Park, MD; (center row, left) Photo by Charles Miller, courtesy *Fine Homebuilding* magazine, © The Taunton Press, Inc.; design: Alan Jencks, Berkeley, CA; (center row, right) Photo © Michael Dunne, courtesy Elizabeth Whiting Associates, London, England; design: Andrew-Usiskin, London, England; (bottom row, far left) Photo © Barry Halkin; (bottom row, second from left) Photo © Alan Geller; design: John Rohosky, Architecture and Construction, San Francisco, CA; (bottom row, far right) Photo by Charles Bickford, courtesy *Fine Homebuilding* magazine, © The Taunton Press, Inc.; design: James Stageberg, Minneapolis, MN.

front flap: (top left) Photo © Claudio Santini; (top right) Photo © E. Andrew McKinney; (bottom left) Photo © Mark Lohman Photography; design: Quentin Dart Parker; (bottom right) Photo © John Sutton; design: Brayton & Hughes Design Studio, San Francisco, CA.

back flap: (top) Photo © Lang Photo; (bottom) Photo © davidduncanlivingston.com.

title page spread: Photo © Mark Lohman Photography; design: Quentin Dart Parker.

table of contents: (left to right) Photos © Jeff Allen, Edward Addeo, Brian Vanden Brink, Peter Mauss/Esto Photographics, Inc., Dan Cornish, Brian Vanden Brink, Carolyn L. Bates.

p. 2: Photo © John Sutton; design: Brayton & Hughes Design Studio, San Francisco, CA.

p. 3: Photo © Carolyn L. Bates; restoration: Billings Farm and Museum, Woodstock, VT.

p. 4: (top) Photo © Grey Crawford; design: Antonio Da Motta Leal, NY; (bottom) Photo © Grey Crawford; design: Lou Ann Bauer, San Francisco, CA.

p. 5: Photo © Tim Austin; design: Zimmerman Architects, West Hartford, CT.

p. 6: Photo © Jeffrey Allen; design: Bentley and Churchill, Architects, Nantucket, MA.

p. 8: (top) Photo © Dale Mulfinger; design: Georgia Bizios, Bizios Architects, Chapel Hill, NC; (bottom) Photo © Jamie Salomon.

p. 9: Photo © Brian Vanden Brink.

p. 11: Photo © Mark Lohman Photography; design: Quentin Dart Parker.

p. 12: Photo by Grey Crawford, © The Taunton Press, Inc.; design: Sharon Tyler Hoover, Architect, Fayetteville, AR.

p. 13: (top) Photo © Barbara Bourne; design: Gene Callahan, Black Oak General Contracting, Fieldbrook, CA; (bottom) Photo © Grey Crawford; design: Clodagh, New York, NY.

p. 14: Photo © davidduncanlivingston.com.

p. 15: (top) Photo © Brian Vanden Brink; (bottom) Photo © Carolyn L. Bates; design: T. Montgomery, Architect, Burlington, VT.

p. 16: (top) Photo © Carolyn L. Bates; (bottom) Photo © Jeffrey Allen; design: Bentley and Churchill, Architects, Nantucket, MA.

p. 17: Photo © Jamie Salomon.

p. 18: (top) Photo © Philip Beaurline; design: Mario Grigni; (bottom left) Photo © Peter Krupenye; design: Carol Kurth Architects, Bedford, NY; (bottom right) Photo © Erhard Pfeiffer.

p. 19: Photo © Claudio Santini.

p. 20: Photo © Carolyn L. Bates.

p. 21: Photo © Steve Vierra Photography.

p. 22: Photo © Brad Simmons/Esto Photographics, Inc.

p. 23: (right) Photo © Tim Street-Porter; (left) Photo © davidduncanlivingston.com.

p. 24: Photo © Brian Vanden Brink.

p. 25: Photo © davidduncanlivingston.com.

p. 26: (top) Photo © Grey Crawford; chest design: Berkeley Mills; (bottom) Photo by Grey Crawford, © The Taunton Press, Inc.; design: SALA Architects, Minneapolis, MN.

p. 27: Photo © Tim Street-Porter.

p. 28: (top) Photo © Peter Aaron/Esto Photographics, Inc.; design: James Cutler; (bottom) Photo © Tim Street-Porter.

p. 29: Photo © Steve Vierra Photography; builder: The Sullivan Company, Newton, MA.

p. 30: Photo © E. Andrew McKinney.

p. 31: Photo © Sandy Agrafiotis.

p. 32: Photo © Dan Cornish; design: Austin Patterson Disston Architects, Southport, CT.

p. 33: (top) Photo © Alan Geller; design: John Rohosky, Architecture and Construction, San Francisco, CA; (bottom) Photo © Philip Beaurline; design: Travis Price Architects, Takoma Park, MD.

p. 35: Photo © Brian Vanden Brink.

p. 37: (top left) Photo © Roger Brooks; (top right) Photo © Claudio Santini; (bottom) Photo © Erhard Pfeiffer.

p. 38: Photo © Barry Halkin.

p. 39: Photo © Roger Brooks.

p. 40: (top) Photo © Claudio Santini; (bottom) Photo © Melabee M. Miller Photography.

p. 41: Photo © Philip Beaurline; design: Travis Price Architects, Takoma Park, MD.

p. 42: Photo © by Edward Addeo; design: Bebe Winkler Interior Design, New York, NY.

p. 43: Photo by davidduncanlivingston.com, © The Taunton Press, Inc.; design; Jean Steinbrecher, Langley, WA.

pp. 44–45: Photos by Scott Gibson, courtesy *Fine Homebuilding* magazine, © The Taunton Press, Inc.

p. 46: (top) Photo © davidduncanlivingston.com; (bottom) Photo © Grey Crawford.

p. 47: Photos © John Sutton; design: Brayton & Hughes Design Studio, San Francisco, CA.

p. 48: Photo © Claudio Santini.

p. 49: Photos © Anne Gummerson Photography; design: Mike Bowers, Design Alternatives.

p. 50: Photo © Tim Street-Porter.

p. 51: (left) Photo © Michael Dunne, courtesy Elizabeth Whiting Associates, London, England; design: Borus and Borus; (right) Photo by Steve Culpepper, courtesy *Fine Homebuilding* magazine, © The Taunton Press, Inc.; design: Jon Anderson, Albuquerque, NM.

p. 52: Photo © Melabee M. Miller Photography.

p. 53: (top) Photo © Phillip H. Ennis Photography; (bottom) Photo © Grey Crawford.

p. 54: Photos by Charles Miller, courtesy *Fine Homebuilding* magazine, © The Taunton Press, Inc.; design: Dennis Wedlick, New York, NY.

p. 55: Photo by davidduncanlivingston.com, © The Taunton Press, Inc.; design: Hiner-Carson Architects, Port Townsend, WA.

p. 56: Photo © Mark Lohman Photography.

p. 57: (top left) Photo by Grey Crawford, © The Taunton Press, Inc.; design: Barry Svigals, New Haven, CT; (top right) Photo courtesy General Electric; (bottom) Photo © Roger Turk/Northlight Photography.

p. 58: Photo by Andy Engel, courtesy *Fine Homebuilding* magazine, © The Taunton Press, Inc.; design: Ken Dahlin.

p. 59: (top) Photo © Keith A. Swan/ Esto Photographics, Inc.; (bottom) Photo © Grey Crawford; design: Katina Arts Meyer, NY.

p. 60: (left) Photo © Melabee M. Miller Photography; (right) Photo © davidduncanlivingston.com; design: Miller Stein.

p. 61: (top) Photo © Tim Street-Porter; design: Tom Callaway, Brentwood, CA; (bottom) Photo © Barry Halkin.

pp. 62–63: Photos © Barbara Bourne; design: Gene Callahan, Black Oak General Contracting, Fieldbrook, CA.

p. 64: Photo © Tria Giovan.

p. 65: (top left) Photo © davidduncanlivingston.com; (bottom left) Photo © Grey Crawford; (right) Photo © John Sutton; design: Brayton & Hughes Design Studio, San Francisco, CA.

p. 66: Photo © Brian Vanden Brink.

p. 67: Photo by Grey Crawford, © The Taunton Press, Inc.; design: SALA Architects, Stillwater, MN.

p. 68: Photo © Melabee M. Miller Photography; design: Elizabeth Gillin.

p. 69: (left) Photo © davidduncanlivingston.com; (right) Photo © Willow Ayers; design: George Suyama Architects, Seattle, WA.

p. 70: Photo © E. Andrew McKinney; design: Brayton & Hughes Design Studio, San Francisco, CA.

p. 71: (top) Photo © Michael Dunne, courtesy Elizabeth Whiting Associates, London, England; design: Barry Goralnick; (bottom left and right) Photos by Charles Miller, courtesy *Fine Homebuilding* magazine, © The Taunton Press, Inc.; design: William Dutcher, Berkeley, CA.

p. 72: (top) Photo © davidduncanlivingston.com. (bottom) Photo by Grey Crawford, © The Taunton Press, Inc.; design: Jacobson Silverstein Winslow, Architects, Berkeley, CA.

p. 73: Photos © davidduncanlivingston.com.

pp. 74–75: Photos © Peter Krupenye; design: Carol Kurth Architects.

p. 76: Photos © Willow Ayers; design: George Suyama Architects, Seattle, WA.

p. 77: Photos © Michael Dunne, courtesy Elizabeth Whiting Associates, London, England; design: Clodagh.

p. 78: Photos © Grey Crawford; design: Janine Wong, Boston, MA.

p. 79: Photos © Anne Gummerson Photography; design: William Lupton.

p. 80: Photo © Tim Street-Porter; design: Nick Berman, Brentwood, CA.

p. 81: Photos by Grey Crawford, © The Taunton Press. Inc.; design: DWH Architects, Taos, NM.

p. 82: Photos © Mark Darley/Esto Photographics, Inc.; design: Patricia Motzkin Architecture, Berkeley, CA.

p. 83: (top) Photo © Tria Giovan; design: Mary Selover; (bottom) Photo © Roger Turk/Northlight Photography.

p. 84: Photos by Andy Engel, courtesy *Fine Homebuilding* magazine, © The Taunton Press, Inc.; design: Brendan R. Coburn.

p. 85: (left) Photo by Roe A. Osborn, courtesy *Fine Homebuilding* magazine, © The Taunton Press, Inc.; design: Kelly Davis, SALA Architects, Stillwater, MN; (right) Photo © Grey Crawford; design: Steinbomer and Associates, TX.

p. 86: (top) Photo © Jamie Salomon; (bottom) Photo © Roger Turk/ Northlight Photography.

p. 87: (top left, bottom left) Photos by Grey Crawford, © The Taunton Press, Inc.; design: Svigals Associates, New Haven, CT; (right) Photo © Mark Lohman Photography.

p. 88: Photo by Steve Culpepper, courtesy *Fine Homebuilding* magazine, © The Taunton Press, Inc.; design Scott Neely, Lincoln, NE.

p. 89: Photos by Kevin Ireton, courtesy *Fine Homebuilding* magazine, © The Taunton Press, Inc.; design: G. Robert Parker, Halifax, Nova Scotia.

p. 90: Photo © Peter Mauss/Esto Photographics, Inc.; design: Kurth & Kurth Architects/Carol Kurth, AIA, Bedford, NY.

p. 91: Photo © Michael Dunne, courtesy Elizabeth Whiting Associates, London, England; design: Sara Klar.

p. 92: Photo © Susan Rockrise; design: David Baker and Associates, San Francisco, CA.

p. 93: (left) Photo © Claudio Santini; (right) Photo © Melabee M. Miller Photography.

p. 94: Photo © Mark Darley/Esto Photographics, Inc.

p. 95: (left) Photo © Jamie Salomon; (right) Photo © Roger Turk/ Northlight Photography.

pp. 96–97: Photos by Charles Miller, courtesy *Fine Homebuilding* magazine, © The Taunton Press, Inc.; design: Alan Jencks, Berkeley, CA.

p. 98: Photo © Brian Vanden Brink.

p. 99: (top) Photo © Melabee M. Miller Photography; (bottom) Photo © Anne Gummerson Photography; design: Melville-Thomas Architects.

pp. 100–101: Photos © Marty Gunion; design: Penny Gimbel, Chandler, AZ.

p. 102: Photos by Charles Miller, courtesy *Fine Homebuilding* magazine, © The Taunton Press, Inc.; design: Cathi and Steven House, San Francisco, CA.

pp. 103–105: Photos © Douglas Hill; design: Bestor Architecture, Los Angeles, CA.

p. 106: Photo © Anne Gummerson Photography; design and woodwork: ILEX Woodworking.

p. 107: Photo by Steve Culpepper, courtesy *Fine Homebuilding* magazine, © The Taunton Press, Inc.; design: Jon Anderson, Albuquerque, NM.

p. 108: Photo © davidduncanlivingston.com.

p. 109: Photos © Trish Martin; design: Bestor Design Studio, Los Angeles, CA.

pp. 110–111: Photos © Steve Vierra Photography; builder: The Sullivan Company, Newton Highlands, MA.

p. 112: Photo © Michael Dunne, courtesy Elizabeth Whiting Associates, London, England; design: Andrew-Usiskin, London, England.

pp. 113–114: Photos © Tim Austin; design: Zimmerman Architects, West Hartford, CT.

p. 115: (top) Photo © Melabee M. Miller Photography; (bottom left and right) Photos by davidduncanlivingston.com, © The Taunton Press, Inc.; design: Kuklinski + Rappe Architects, Chicago, IL.

p. 116: (left) Photo by Roe A. Osborn, courtesy *Fine Homebuilding* magazine, © The Taunton Press, Inc.; design: James McNeely, Boston, MA; (right) Photo by Grey Crawford, © The Taunton Press, Inc.; design: SALA Architects, Minneapolis, MN.

p. 117: (top left) Photo © Rob Karosis; (top right) Photo courtesy Velux-America; (bottom left) Photo by Charles Miller, courtesy *Fine Homebuilding* magazine, © The Taunton Press, Inc.; design: Jan Wisniewski.

pp. 118–119: Photos by Roe A. Osborn, courtesy *Fine Homebuilding* magazine, © The Taunton Press, Inc.

p. 121: (top) Photo © Dennis Crews; design: Ray Tetz, Silver Spring, MD; (bottom) Photo © E. Andrew McKinney.

pp. 122–123: Photos © Bernard Wolf; design: Bestor Architecture, Los Angeles, CA.

p. 125: Photo © Brian Vanden Brink.

pp. 126–128: Photos © Tom Bonner; design: Kanner Architects, Los Angeles, CA.

pp. 129–130: Photos © Dugan/Powers/Yokum, Photographers; design: Barry Berkus, Santa Barbara, CA.

p. 131: Photo © davidduncanlivingston.com; design: Miller Stein.

p. 132: Photo © Dan Cornish; design: Austin Patterson Disston Architects, Southport, CT.

p. 133: Photo © Rob Karosis; design: Gary Wolf Architects, Boston, MA.

p. 134: Photo © Daniel Doz; design: Eggink Mounayar Architects, Muncie, IN.

p. 135: Photo © Salvador Behar; design: Salvador Behar Architects, Mamaroneck, NY.

p. 136: Photo © Brian Vanden Brink; design: Centerbrook Architects, CT.

pp. 138–139: Photos © Randy O'Rourke; design: William Clark, Patterson, NY.

pp. 140–143: Photos © Dan Cornish; design: Austin Patterson Disston Architects, Southport, CT.

pp. 144–145: Photos © Barbara Bourne; design: Patricia Motzkin, Berkeley, CA.

pp. 146–149: Photos © Philip Beaurline; design: Travis Price Architects, Takoma Park, MD.

pp. 150–151: Photos © Sandy Agrafiotis; design: Anne Whitney, Portsmouth, NH.

pp. 152–153: Photos © Del Brown; design: Joe Mirenna, Madison, WI.

pp. 154–156: Photos © Philip Beaurline; design: Travis Price Architects, Takoma Park, MD.

p. 157: Photos © Carolyn L. Bates; design: Milford Cushman, Cushman and Beckstrom Architecture and Planning, Stowe, VT.

p. 158: Photo © Daniel Doz; design: Eggink Mounayar Architects, Muncie, IN.

pp. 159 and 161: Photos © Sandy Agrafiotis; design: Benjamin Nutter Associates, Topsfield, MA.

pp. 162–163: Photos © Alex Beatty; design: Luna Design Group (Luis Lobao, project manager), Lynnfield, MA; desk design: Barbara Bradlee.

pp. 164–167: Photos © Rob Karosis; design: Gary Wolf Architects, Boston, MA.

pp. 168–169: Photos © Brian Vanden Brink; design: Matt and Libby Elliot, Brooklyn, ME.

p. 170: (top) Photo © Michael Dunne, courtesy Elizabeth Whiting Associates, London, England; design: V. Smith-Durham; (bottom) Photo © Grey Crawford; design: Wayne and Barbara King, Ipswich, MA.

p. 171: (top) Photo © Grey Crawford; (bottom) Photo by Scott Gibson, courtesy *Fine Homebuilding* magazine, © The Taunton Press, Inc.; design: Jock Sewall, Montecito, CA.

p. 172: Photo © Peter Paige.

pp. 174–175: Photos © Alan Geller; design: Kurt Lavenson and Lesly Avedisian, Lavenson Design, Alamo, CA.

pp. 176–177: Photos © Randy O'Rourke; design: Keith Roberts, Jacksonville Beach, FL.

pp. 178–180: Photos © Sloan Howard; design: Don Moyle, Wilton, CT.

pp. 181 and 183: Photos © Rob Karosis; design: Malcolm Ross MacKenzie Architect, West Newton, MA.

pp. 184–185: Photos © Randy O'Rourke; design: Susan Snell, Cooperstown, NY.

pp. 186–187: Photos © Carolyn L. Bates; contractor: Mike Crane, Three Seasons Builders, Burlington, VT.

p. 188: Photos © Philip Beaurline; design: Mario Grigni Architect, Greensboro, NC.

p. 189: Photos © Carolyn L. Bates; design: Kent Eaton, Soho Modular Design, Jericho, VT.

pp. 190–191: Photos © Philip Beaurline; design: Travis Price Architects, Takoma Park, MD.

pp. 192–194: Photos © Philip Beaurline; design: Orin Arvold, The Architects Alliance, Blacksburg, VA.

pp. 195–196: Photos © Alan Geller; design: John Rohosky, San Francisco, CA.

pp. 197, 198 (top), and 199: Photos © Jeffrey Totaro, Tom Crane Photographers; design: John Milner Architects, Chadds Ford, PA.

p. 198: (bottom) Photo © Andre Harvey.

pp. 200–201: Photos by Charles Bickford, courtesy *Fine Homebuilding* magazine, © The Taunton Press, Inc.; design: James Stageberg, Minneapolis, MN.

pp. 202–203: Photos © Michael Jensen; design: John and Inga Rouches, Sally Owen.

p. 204: Photo © Carolyn L. Bates; design: Gary Starr, Weybridge, VT.

p. 205: Photo © Sandy Agrafiotis.

p. 206: Photo by Scott Gibson, courtesy *Fine Homebuilding* magazine, © The Taunton Press, Inc.; design: Jock Sewall, Montecito, CA.

p. 207: Photos © E. Andrew McKinney.

p. 208: Photo © Anne Gummerson Photography; design: Sarah Schweizer, Architect.

p. 209: Photo © Jeffrey Allen; design: Bentley and Churchill, Architects, Nantucket, MA.

p. 210: Photo © Jeffrey Totaro, Tom Crane Photographers; design: John Milner Architects, Chadds Ford, PA.

pp. 211–213: Photos © Carolyn L. Bates.

pp. 214–215: Photos © Sandy Agrafiotis.

pp. 216–219: Photos © Jeffrey Allen; design: Bentley and Churchill, Architects, Nantucket, MA.

pp. 220–222: Photos © Carolyn L. Bates; design: Gary Starr, Weybridge, VT.

pp. 223–225: Photos © Carolyn L. Bates; design: Carol MacDonald, Colchester, VT.

pp. 226–227: Photos © Rob Karosis.

pp. 228–231: Photos © Keith Cronin; design: Mark Dziewulski, Sacramento, CA, and London, England.